Beyond Convention

GENRE INNOVATION IN ACADEMIC WRITING

Christine M. Tardy

University of Arizona

Foreword by
Dana R. Ferris

T0350048

Ann Arbor
University of Michigan Press

Some portions of Chapter 4 appear in Tardy, C.M. (2015). Bending genres, or when is a deviation an innovation? In N. Artemeva & A. Freedman (Eds.), *Trends and traditions in genre studies: Beyond the three traditions.* Edmonton, AB: Inkshed Publications.

♾ Printed on acid-free paper

ISBN-13: 978-0-472-03647-9

2019   2018   2017   2016   4   3   2   1

Foreword

By Dana R. Ferris, University of California–Davis

In a 2016 episode (Season 7, Episode 12) of the CBS TV courtroom drama, *The Good Wife*, the main character Alicia Florrick and her partner are representing a singer-songwriter being sued by his recording label for breach of contract. The plaintiff's claim is that the artist's second album is not in the same musical genre (pop music) as his first, thus violating the terms of his agreement with the record company. Both sides bring in their own expert witnesses, music professors at renowned institutions. Here is part of the testimony of the first expert witness, brought by the plaintiff (the recording company):

Plaintiff's Attorney:	Doctor, what is "popular music"?
Expert Witness #1:	A genre of popular music based in rock 'n' roll of the '50s and '60s.
PA:	And how would you recognize a pop song?
EW #1:	Through its hooks. Pop songs are all full of hooks. There's one in the intro, another in the chorus, another in the bridge….
[…]	
PA:	And that's all there is to it? The hooks?
EW #1:	No. Pop songs also tend to be non-harmonic, with pronounced timbrel dissonance, four-bar phrasing, a beat-per-minute range between 72 and 85….
PA:	So you're saying that [name of defendant]'s new album didn't have most of these hallmarks.
EW #1:	I'm saying it had none of them.

After a cross-examination in which Alicia's partner gets the expert witness to admit that the iconic pop song "Bohemian Rhapsody" by Queen violates the specific genre conventions he had just described, the defense puts its own expert witness on the stand:

Defendant's Attorney:	Would you agree that [defendant]'s second album is not in the same pop genre as his first album?
Expert Witness #2:	I don't think I'd agree with any part of that. His first album wasn't exactly 100% pop, and I don't think his second is all that different.
DA:	Can you explain?
EW #2:	Well, yeah. Genres aren't fixed, right? They ebb and flow over time, and then there's this give and take between genres.
[...]	
DA:	So is this the same or different than [name of another song written by defendant]?
EW #2:	I don't know....it's both, man. [Defendant]'s an artist. He's exploring. Both those songs are written by the same person, but they're not identical. And no album should be identical, like Picasso...you see him going through his Blue Period or his Crystal Period....

This exchange about music captures in a nutshell Christine Tardy's argument in this new book on *genre innovation*: Genres are recognizable because they do have characteristics and boundaries, but genres "aren't fixed" and "they ebb and flow over time." A third and critical part of her argument is that neither genre constraints nor innovations are objective realities by themselves; they may be accepted or rejected depending upon the larger social system into which they are introduced. Thus, "Bohemian Rhapsody," despite its violating of pop music genre boundaries, is widely accepted as being a pop song—and its innovation arguably is what makes it stand out as a hit.

What does all of this mean for genre researchers and writing instructors? That is the question with which I approached reading this book. With the exception of a few pages in a book chapter I wrote several years ago (Ferris, 2011), I am not a researcher of or expert on genre. However, I am a genre *practitioner*. Beyond the obvious—I consume and produce a wide range of written genres as an academic writer, editor, teacher, and social media user—I have enthusiastically adopted genre pedagogy in my own teaching of writing and in curriculum development as a writing program administrator in several different roles: as a first-year writing director, as the director of a large developmental writing program for multilingual students, and as a teacher of advanced writing courses for upper-division and graduate students.

Tardy's book has something for everyone. For genre scholars, the first several chapters carefully lay the groundwork and present a theoretical framework for examining both genre theory and genre innovation, and the final chapter outlines directions for further research on innovation. For hands-on genre researchers, Chapter 4 presents a compelling narrative of Tardy's own primary research on genre innovation and how it is both encouraged and discouraged by a professor in an environmental science class for students preparing to research and write their senior theses. This chapter is especially notable because the research (like all of Tardy's empirical work) is carefully designed and explained and engagingly described, so it is a good model for classroom writing researchers in general and genre researchers in particular. This chapter was also extremely interesting for me as I further envisioned how genre instruction in a writing class might better prepare students for a wide range of disciplinary writing innovations.

For classroom teachers, though, Chapter 5 is the real payoff. As I mentioned, I am already an enthusiastic genre practitioner as a teacher, program administrator, and teacher educator, but I got some great new practical ideas for teaching from this chapter—not only about how better to present genre awareness/knowledge concepts but especially about authentic and organic ways to introduce the notion of innovation (which Tardy also calls "genre play") into the writing course syllabus. I am already imagining how my own advanced composition course (which is based on building genre awareness and genre knowledge for upper-division university students from a wide range of disciplines) will benefit from the added insights of this chapter.

Until I read this book, I didn't realize how much I myself enjoy genre innovation, both as a consumer and as a writer. One of my current favorite Twitter accounts to follow is a parody account known as @manwhohasitall. Its anonymous author tweets pithy bits of advice and inspiration to busy working husbands and fathers that imitate the kinds of "wisdom" that women's publications (magazines, websites, blogs, etc.) try to impart so that women can "have it all"—juggle the demands of a spouse, children, a career, a household, and health and physical perfection. Here are a couple of examples from the Twitter account:

> From Jan. 24, 2016: "The plight of the over-committed dad remains an epidemic. Try getting up an hour earlier than you wife & kids to get everything done."

> From Jan. 19, 2016: "FRAZZLED working dad? Curl up on the sofa in your pjs with a plain yoghurt, half a walnut and a good book. 'Me time.'"

Reading this Twitter account, one quickly realizes how ridiculous such advice sounds when it is aimed at men rather than women. It successfully mimics the genre of "advice to busy working wives/mothers" so that it is recognizable but then "innovates" by changing the target audience from men to women. The great success of this Twitter account (its author is now getting invitations to publish humorous "advice columns" for men in newspapers) attests to both sides of Tardy's argument in the book: The parody works because the genre is recognizable, and the innovation is well received by its audience of Twitter followers (more than 100,000 at the time of this writing).

Not only do I enjoy genre innovation, I also participate in it as a writer. In Chapter 3, Tardy talks about the ways different types of innovation have emerged in usually stodgy academic writing genres. Reading this chapter, I realized that I myself have produced some of these genre innovations, most notably autobiographical chapters or portions of chapters (e.g., detailing my journey as a researcher or my experiences as an applied linguist). I also became aware that in my own writing and in my work with student writers, I tend to resist convention and encourage innovation. For example, my PhD students would attest that I am always reminding them to make their writing more accessible by avoiding passive voice and excessively long sentences, and by minimizing jargon or at least defining their terms in context. I have often encouraged students to bring first-person narratives into their academic writing as well. Finally, of course, in the spirit of the book I am introducing, I have chosen to write this foreword in a rather innovative way(!).

Reading this book did more than just make me more aware of something I already, somewhat subconsciously, was doing, however. It pushed my thinking about if, when, and how writing teachers should encourage students to push genre boundaries and to innovate. I came away convinced that I need to do more to explicitly teach this and to intentionally ask students to experiment. Without genre innovation, we do risk (as Tardy notes) falling into deadening, formulaic views of and approaches to teaching genre knowledge and are painting only a partial picture of genre for our students.

NOTE

Permission to use @manwhohasitall tweets granted by United Agents LLP.

REFERENCE

Ferris, D.R. (2011). Written discourse analysis and L2 teaching. In E. Hinkel (Ed.), *Handbook of research in second language teaching and learning*, Vol. II (pp. 643–662). New York: Routledge/Taylor & Francis.

Contents

Acknowledgments

Though presented in a finished form, this book represents a work-in-progress that began in my head—and research notes—at least as far back as 2006. I am grateful to DePaul University and the College of Liberal Arts and Social Sciences for a summer research grant and quarter-long research leave that contributed greatly to this project, and for the opportunity to participate in the 2010 Connected Communities Summer Seminar, which provided me the luxury of thinking about changes and tipping points from systems-based perspectives with colleagues across the disciplines.

Special thanks also goes to "Professor Hanson" and her Research Methods students (especially Brooke, Eileen, Frank, and Kurt—all pseudonyms) for allowing me into their classroom and sharing their ideas and writing with me (described in Chapter 4), and to Mark Lazio for his research assistance in analyzing some of the data from that study. Thank you as well to Pat Maher and Youngju Park for use of their wedding invitation (Figure 1.2) and to Juan Tauber for use of his paper (Figures 5.4 and 5.5) in Chapter 5.

I also need to thank the many people who have influenced and challenged my thinking on issues of genre innovation and creativity, through personal and in-print conversations—there are too many to mention here, but their names are clear in my reference list. As well, I thank the many multilingual writing students I have had over the years who have raised my own awareness of the complexities of genre; the graduate students in my spring 2015 genre seminar for inspiring me through their innovative approaches to genre; and Deborah Crusan, Madelyn Tucker Pawlowski, Jenny Slinkard, Todd Ruecker, Sarah Read, and Lisa Dush for their valuable feedback on portions of this book. I am also very indebted to John Swales for reading and commenting on an early draft of several chapters and for his continued support and encouragement with the project. And I am extremely appreciative of Ann Johns' thoughtful reading and feedback, which challenged and developed my thinking on pedagogy—an area of genre studies that I continue to wrestle with.

I am especially grateful to Kelly Sippell of University of Michigan Press, who understood the delays in this book prompted by a baby, a cross-country move, and a new job, and nevertheless stuck with me; her encouragement, support, and flexibility were critical in completing the project. On that note, I am also very thankful to my husband, Matthew, and for little Benny, both of whom have pushed my thinking on the value of challenging and disrupting genre norms, each in their own way.

Introduction

For many years now, I've kept in my office a growing collection of genre samples made up of texts I can use with students to explore genre through representative artifacts. It started as a collection of wedding invitations, thanks to Johns' (1997) suggestion that these offer an excellent springboard for introducing students to genre. Eventually, I started adding other interesting genres that I came across, such as charity donation request letters, political campaign flyers, spam emails, and bad-news memos from university administrators. Always on the lookout for new texts for my collection, I became particularly interested in off-beat instances of genres, like the lease-renewal letter shared in Figure 1.1 of this book or the wedding invitation in Figure 1.2 (a–c). These texts, it seemed to me, demonstrated the power of convention . . . by breaking from it.

Genre theory has long acknowledged variation as inherent to genre, with theoretical discussions typically mentioning the possibilities for creativity, disruption, or flouting of convention. As a reader, I found myself repeatedly underlining such comments in notable texts but always wanting a bit more. What actually *were* the possibilities for writers, and particularly student writers? It is not uncommon, after all, to hear teachers remark that "students must show that they know the rules before they can break them." While struggling with questions of why, when, and how different writers can manipulate conventions, I became increasingly interested in related research into voice and identity in academic writing. Scholarship in this area has offered interesting insight into how individuals present themselves in unique ways within available generic options (Hyland, 2012; Matsuda, 2001), and research has also highlighted *readers'* roles in constructing author identities (Matsuda & Tardy, 2007; Tardy & Matsuda, 2009). In conducting a study of voice in student writing, I became intrigued by how the same features of a student's text could be read by one teacher as a sign of a developing writer and by another as a sign of a creative and confident writer (Tardy, 2012b). Readers clearly play a pivotal role in characterizing texts and writers as deviant or innovative, but it also seemed that genre, setting, roles, and relations were relevant as well.

While my encounters with "real genres" and engagement with writing scholarship were both instrumental in the genesis of this book, it has perhaps been my work as a writing teacher and teacher educator that has had the most impact on my thinking. I am particularly attentive to critiques of genre pedagogy that caution that genres may be perceived by students (and teachers) as templates or formulas and that conventions may be interpreted as rules; I have seen this potential in my own classrooms as I struggle to engage students in the dynamic, social nuances of a text that they are experiencing out of context and as a graded assignment. Yet, I remain convinced that genre offers a valuable tool for writing students and teachers to explore expected conventions as well as the possibilities for quirky or transformative innovations—that is, the possibilities for real engagement in the processes of written communication. This book attempts to engage directly with these complexities and tensions in genre from both theoretical and pedagogical perspectives.

With writing and writers as its focus, *Beyond Convention* draws on relevant scholarship across disciplines, looking most heavily to work in applied linguistics and writing studies. Together, these fields offer tools for blending systematic analysis of text with rich understandings of how texts shape and are shaped by sociopolitical contexts—both vital pieces of genre innovation. I adopt Lemke's (1993) metaphor of ecosocial systems as a framework for bringing these pieces together and highlighting the dynamic and inter-related features that influence how language is used and how it is evaluated by others. With an interdisciplinary spirit, I have also tried to make the terminology and descriptions throughout the book accessible to a range of readers.

Adopting an interdisciplinary approach is also valuable for understanding genre innovation in ways that are inclusive of diverse writers and writing contexts. Toward that aim, this book considers a range of learning and teaching settings, including first-year undergraduate writing, undergraduate writing in the disciplines, and the advanced academic writing of graduate students and professionals. While my discussions will not be tied to first language or multilingual writing, I hope that they might be informative to both. At the same time, I acknowledge that my interpretations and explorations are bound by my own experiences, which have been predominantly in teaching adults in higher education.

As should by now be clear, this book is intended for those interested in the complexities of written communication, whether their interests are grounded in genre theory, academic discourse, discourse analysis, or writing instruction. With its attentiveness to context, discipline, and community, it offers a resource for those interested in English for Academic Purposes, English for Specific Purposes, and Writing in the Disciplines. At its heart, this is a book for teachers and teacher educators, though I hope it can inform our research and theoretical work as well. In the end, perhaps the discussions and examples in the book can inspire us to think of the potential for innovation in academic writing and writing instruction, while also keeping a close eye on the very real constraints that are at play for novice writers.

Chapter Overview

Chapter 1 situates this book within a larger conversation of genre and the heteroglossic nature of written communication. This chapter offers a working definition of genre innovation as effective departures from convention, and it explores examples of innovation in a range of non-academic genres. The chapter concludes with an argument for an extended study of genre innovation particularly in the context of academic writing.

In Chapter 2, I explore research on innovation and creativity from fields like rhetoric and composition, pragmatics, applied linguistics, and psychology. The chapter then turns to the related issue of identity, highlighting research on writer identity, ethos, voice, and symbolic capital to demonstrate how these issues may influence readers' perceptions of effective innovation within a text. These discussions are followed by a synthesis of major theoretical principles of genre innovation and an application of these principles to a short analysis of an unconventional text. The chapter concludes with an overview of methodologies for studying genre innovation, focusing particularly on the value of methods that examine social context and reception.

Chapter 3 turns to the specific context of academic writing. Carrying over much of the conceptual work developed in the first two chapters, this chapter considers the functions that innovation may carry out in academic contexts, and it offers numerous illustrations from a range of disciplines. This chapter then turns to the task of sketching out a framework or heuristic for exploring some of the ecosocial elements that can shape possibilities for, impediments to, and the nature of innovation in academic genres.

The framework developed in Chapter 3 is put into play in Chapter 4, which shares a study of an undergraduate research class in environmental science. Through an examination of course discussions, student and teacher interviews, and student writing, I explore how genre innovation and creativity are constructed and valued in the process of teaching disciplinary writing and research. By exploring a context of disciplinary acculturation and learning as an ecosocial system, the chapter highlights how the classroom conditions possibilities for genre innovation by disciplinary novices.

In Chapter 5, I turn directly to the role of genre innovation in the academic writing classroom. The chapter explores how research into language play, creativity, and genre awareness suggests that genre play and manipulation can hold a valuable learning function. The latter half of this chapter offers principles and practices for incorporating innovation as a means of building both genre knowledge and genre awareness, including numerous examples that could be adapted to different teaching settings.

Finally, Chapter 6 draws out the main conclusions from the book and their implications for learning and teaching academic writing. It ends with a discussion of potential future directions of inquiry into genre innovation.

Chapter 1

Why Innovation?

Written genres have been described in metaphors as seemingly contrary as straitjackets and playgrounds, tools and life forms, institutions and constellations. In an effort to better understand the so-called genres of power that characterize academic and professional communication, research since the 1980s has carried out text analyses, textographies, case studies, ethnographies, and rhetorical analyses, helping to raise awareness of the common conventions of such texts and how those conventions have come to be. Yet, despite a pervasive acknowledgment that genres are neither static nor rigid, less attention has been paid to the diversity in genres, the innovations that are possible within specific settings. Even when working largely within conventions, both novice and experienced writers often find ways to bend, flout, break, and even transform the regular patterns that characterize generic communication. Sometimes these manipulations fall flat, but other times they are recognized as successful and they allow writers to do things that may not be possible through stricter adherence to conventional patterns. Innovation is ultimately the source of diversity and change in an otherwise relatively stable system. This book is about such innovation, particularly as it plays out in the realm of academic writing, where writers, teachers, and researchers may be more likely to focus on conformity to, rather than departure from, preferred convention. But before jumping into the proverbial water, I begin by re-visiting the role of convention in genre.

Genre and Convention

> "The study of genres has to be founded on the study of convention."
>
> —*Frye, 1957, cited in Miller, 1984, p. 152*

> "Genres encourage choice because their constraints are given."
>
> —*Devitt, 2004, p. 154*

It is not at all surprising—or misguided—for theories of genre to focus on the recognizable, repeated patterns of similar texts. After all, genres are defined primarily in terms of such recognizability and repeatability, as in Miller's (1984) characterization of genres as typified rhetorical action or Hyland's (2000) description of genres as containing "a typical clustering of conventions—developed over time in response to what writers perceive as a similar problem" (p. 5). Kress (1993) explained the existence of these patterns in terms of *regularity*:

> In any society there are regularly recurring situations in which a number of people interact to perform or carry out certain tasks. When these are accompanied by language, of whatever kind, the regularity of the situation will give rise to regularities in the texts which are produced in that situation. (p. 27)

Through participation, we come to recognize these repeated situations and draw on our previous experiences in producing each response. The conventions of a wedding invitation, for example, respond to the need to inform others of the event and to do so in a way that is fitting for the occasion itself—the definition of what is "fitting" is to some extent individual but also shaped within the social worlds we live in. The regularities or conventions of genres are what lead to our perceptions of genres as relatively stable (at least for the moment) actions; we assign labels and roles to them, and they become a part of what we do and how we think about what we do. We know that they change and vary, that we have some freedom to produce, for example, a wedding invitation that is in some way unique, but we tend not to stray too far from expectations when making such choices. After all, in most cases, we want others to recognize our actions as carrying out the function we intended.

Recognition of a text as carrying out a function in a socially preferred way means recognizing the text as a genre. On the one hand, genres allow us to organize and classify our vast experiences in the world and therefore make sense of them. This classificatory aspect of genre has made it a useful research tool in areas like folklore studies or anthropology (Paltridge, 1997; Swales, 1990). Genre theory in applied linguistics and rhetoric and composition studies has taken up the issue of classification in various ways. In rhetorical theory, categorization of genres has been of relatively little interest, but, following Miller (1984), most rhetoricians would distinguish genres by the rhetorical action they aim to carry out rather than by their textual form. In contrast, genre theory as it has developed within systemic functional linguistics (SFL) is more invested in categorizing texts into a priori genres, with the specific aim of addressing educational concerns. By grouping texts into genres and sequencing genres in particular ways, SFL educationists aim to scaffold literacy instruction, gradually apprenticing students into specialized discourses (Martin, 2002).

One approach to genre categorization that strikes something of a middle ground between a strict taxonomy and extreme fluidity is frame semantics (see Paltridge, 1997, for a full discussion of genre and frames). Frames can be thought of as skeletal representations of the world that serve to guide perceptions and actions; they help us perceive order out of the relative chaos of human life. Frame semantics draws on the concept of prototype as a way to understand the fuzzy nature of categorization. Swales' (1990) discussion of genre also turns to prototype as a way to understand variation within genres. In essence, the theory argues that we assign objects, people, or concepts to categories based on their resemblance to an imagined prototype. An object does not need to be identical to the prototype in order to be assigned to its category, but it needs to share enough features (or "family resemblances") with the prototype that it may be thought of as a member. These shared features are referred to in genre theory as *conventions*.

For those interested in language and writing instruction, helping writers identify convention can serve as an important learning tool, a way to demystify the often mysterious worlds of academic or professional writing. Although they differ from rules in their flexibility and social nature, conventions can serve as a familiar crux for both students and more experienced writers, providing a schema (or frame) for production. Without the presence of convention, the notion of genre would arguably be less useful to the study and teaching of writing; indeed, without conventions, we would not have genres.

Yet, despite this important attention to patterns and regularity, genre theory has long demonstrated more than a little unease with a strict focus on sameness and tradition, acknowledging that viewing genres *too much* in terms of their conventions carries the real risk of equating them with de-contextualized templates or formulas, patterns that writers can simply plug in with minor modifications. One of the strongest criticisms against genre-based pedagogies has been that "teaching genres" can easily become or be perceived as teaching formulaic text types. It is perhaps this risk that has led so many theorists to describe genres through adjectives like *changeable, dynamic,* or *stabilized-for-now,* or metaphorically as *life forms, agents,* or *actants.*

In other words, variation and fluidity are also essential characteristics of genre that must be accounted for. After all, examples of a single genre are never identical even within a local space or at a specific point in time. As Miller (1984) notes, the rhetorical situations to which genres respond do not recur in any material sense—what recurs is "our construal of a type" (p. 157). Genres are, thus, "both repeated and constantly revised" (Johns, 2002a, p. 238), as any generic act involves "some degree of innovation" (Hyland, 2000, p. 4). Put another way, any given "typified response" displays both *some adherence* to a norm (thus classifying it as typified) and *some variation* from that norm. Bakhtin (1981) referred to these opposing tendencies in terms of the "unitary language" (the result of centripetal, unifying forces) and "heteroglossia" (resulting from centrifugal, stratifying forces) that co-exist within every utterance. Picking up on Bakhtin's concepts, Devitt (2004) likens generic norms and variation to language norms and variation. Both genre and language standards develop out of social structures, acting as stabilizing forces as they shape social attitudes. When a standard is established, it tends to be repeated and eventually becomes normalized, perhaps even unnoticed until norms are violated. Yet, as Devitt argues, standards (and conventions) rely on the possibility of variation, and they may even enable innovation. After all, without a norm, we cannot have departures; without departures, we cannot have innovation.

What Is "Genre Innovation"?

The notion of innovation brings with it images of newness—new technologies, new visions, new insights. The words *innovation* and *innovative* are often found in mission statements, logos, and peer review criteria, demonstrating the high value placed on work and ideas that are perceived as new. Innovation is often coupled with creativity, and both notions seem to share a similar expression of novelty that is viewed as highly successful. Amabile (1988), for example, defines innovation as "the successful implementation of creative ideas within an organization" (p. 126).

Applied to genre, we tend to relate innovation to change and departure from norms in ways that are perhaps more radical than the variation that already characterizes genre. Fairclough (1992) likens innovation and creativity to "adapting existing conventions in new ways" (p. 96), and Devitt (2004) relates genre creativity to variation, choice, and critique. Definitions of genre innovation are rarely articulated in scholarship, but because the notion is central to this book, I will share in some detail my own use of the term. At the most basic level, I use genre innovation to describe *departures from genre convention that are perceived as effective and successful by the text's intended audience or community of practice.* Focusing momentarily on just the first part of that definition, we can understand departures as potentially occurring at multiple levels. On the surface of a text, we might find relatively simple stylistic departures, such as the use of informal elements like exclamation points or even emoticons (! ☺) in a formal text. But departures also go well beyond these smaller textual elements. Writers can omit or re-sequence traditional move structures of a genre, as examined in Belcher's (1997, 2009) study of the "explicit gap statement" in research article introductions, or writers might mix genres and discourses, resulting in overtly hybridized texts like "infomercials" or "mockumentaries" or in more covert manipulations such as the use of persuasive discourse in corporate reports (Bhatia, 2004). Writers may also carry out genres in innovative ways, as in the example of crowdfunding, whereby individuals or organizations request project funds from the public via internet sites like Kickstarter.com or Indiegogo.com rather than relying on more traditional funding from investors. In some cases, innovation may even lead us to question the genre that a text belongs to, possibly giving rise to new genre categories. Again, these kinds of innovations depend on assumptions that a set of conventions already exist—in other words, the existence of conventions is necessary for departures to be noticeable, noteworthy, and new. Thinking back for a moment to our discussion of frames and prototypes, innovative instances of a genre are often less prototypical, at least in some respects, though their distance from the prototype will vary.

Indeed, genre theorists have already explored metaphors of genre that emphasize their diverse and changing nature over their stability, touching on issues of innovation. Schryer (2011) has offered the metaphor of improvisation as a way to describe the playful and individual variation that occurs within genres. Improvisation has also proven a fruitful area of inquiry for psychologists researching creativity—an area I will take up in greater detail in Chapter 2. The key to this analogy (genre-as-improvisation) lies in the fact that improv, for example in jazz music, is not actually a free-for-all. Rather, as creativity research has noted, jazz musicians work within a set of shared conventions, without which they would not be able to co-perform (Sawyer, 2012). Like Schryer, Devitt (2011) too finds value in adding the notion of *play* to genre theory, considering the potential of viewing genre as a playground. This metaphor, she argues, can serve as a conceptual tool for moving away from more rigid conceptions of genre and situating writers (and writing students in particular) as active inventors rather than passive users.

The metaphors of improv and playgrounds are certainly attractive on one level. They encourage us to see the inventive and creative possibilities in genre, including genres as serious and presumably traditional as academic texts, and they place agency directly in the hands, or keyboards, of writers. Yet, there is a certain limitation to these metaphors as well, as they do not readily account for the power structures inherent in genres, structures that prevent equal access to the resources that allow for writers' choices and potential for play. It also seems likely that, as Bhatia (2006) has pointed out, not all genres are equally amenable to innovation or manipulation. He posits that genres lie on a continuum of "liberal" to "conservative," in which some genres (e.g., professional or legal texts) are subject to more constraints to variation while others (e.g., literary texts) place high value on innovation. A study of genre and innovation, then, needs to account for, on the one hand, writers' agency and their playful manipulations of genres and, on the other, the unifying forces that may discourage such manipulations and that are marked by unequal structures of power.

This consideration of power and reception, then, returns us to the latter part of my definition of genre innovation: To be deemed "innovative," a text must not only depart from convention but also *be perceived as effective and successful by the text's intended audience or community of practice*. Perceptions and judgments are critical to innovation, and it is for this reason that I have not focused on the writer's intention as central to my definition but rather have emphasized the uptake or reception of the generic act. The extent to which such innovative texts lie at the "outer boundaries" of a genre category or frame may ultimately have some effect on how readers judge them, as might various social and political features of the community in which the genre is produced and distributed. How far, for example, can a research article deviate from an imagined prototype before readers (including peer reviewers or editors) assign it to a new category? To what extent can a student writer violate convention and still be given an acceptable grade? As Hamilton and Pitt (2009) remind us, challenging genre conventions means challenging the genre's purpose—often a risky endeavor, to be sure. We will consider, in Chapter 2, some theoretical tools for examining readers' judgment of a genre as innovative or, in contrast, deviant or transgressive. At this point, though, I turn to a more thorough exploration of possibilities for genre innovation.

Innovating Genres

A good starting place for studying genre innovation is examining more precisely where and how writers might innovate. To study genre innovation empirically, including not just the products but also the processes of production and reception, we need a model or framework to work from. In their study of the writing of university undergraduates and faculty members, Thaiss and Zawacki (2006) outline a taxonomy of "alternatives" in academic writing that considers several levels of potential innovation: formats, ways of conceptualizing and arranging academic arguments, syntaxes, methodologies, and media. This taxonomy usefully goes beyond stylistic alternatives to much more conceptual forms of innovation, so it certainly has heuristic value. At the same time, a model firmly grounded in genre theory may be more appropriate for understanding how such innovation may operate within and through *genres*. Research into genre knowledge offers a potentially productive heuristic for studying genre innovation, as innovation depends on knowledge of convention.

While scholars have offered slightly different descriptions of genre knowledge (e.g., Beaufort, 2004; Berkenkotter & Huckin, 1995; Bhatia, 1999; Hyland, 2004), most bring knowledge of form and rhetorical strategies together with knowledge of the content and processes used to carry out the genre in coordination with related genres (e.g., Tardy, 2009). Relating innovation to these areas of genre knowledge allows us to see where a text may depart from the expectations of gatekeepers and others. Departures may be found, for example, in the language style adopted, the arrangement of ideas, or the kinds of evidence a writer uses. But beyond form and rhetorical strategies, a writer may create a text that develops content in surprising or novel ways or may carry out a genre through new methodologies or practices considered innovative or even path-breaking. Some examples, not limited to academic writing, may be useful to illustrate the potential of this framework.

A fairly straightforward instance of stylistic (or formal) innovation in a genre is found in Figure 1.1, a lease-renewal letter I received several years ago from the management company of the apartment I was living in at the time. Initially, the letter appears quite conventional,

Figure 1.1. Lease-Renewal Letter

May 3, 2005

Christine Tardy
5556 N. Lakewood #G3
Chicago, IL 60640

Dear Christine,

Your existing lease is expiring on 7/31/2005 and we hope you have enjoyed living in a 606 Property.

Enclosed you will find two documents:

  1. Lease Extension Agreement (2)
  2. Intent to Vacate Notice

We truly, truly, truly hope you decide to stay with us but we also understand that residents eventually have to move. Should you decide not to renew, we will be very sad and require extensive psychological therapy, so please renew.

pretty much what readers would anticipate in this genre; it is not until the third paragraph that we find humorous and unexpected language, clearly flouting traditional conventions both in terms of language style and content. This text also offers a good example of innovations to the rhetorical strategies typically used in the genre. By mockingly appealing to emotion ("we will be very sad and require extensive psychological therapy"), the letter departs radically from the more common appeals to logic (or even lack of any obvious persuasive strategies) that might be found in such a letter.

A second example also illustrates departures to generic form, rhetorical strategies, and content, but in an even more extensive manner. Following Ann Johns' (1997) discussion of "homely" genres that can provide a useful starting point for introducing students to the notion of genre, I frequently use wedding invitations as a springboard for discussions of genre in my writing classes. Over the years, I have amassed a nice collection of this genre with variations to color, size, formality, language, social practice, and ideology, but recently a student shared with me a wedding invitation she had received that was by far the most innovative I had seen. The invitation itself, partially displayed in Figure 1.2 (a–c), has four panels that fold out, obliging readers to interact with it in ways much different from a traditional invitation. From the top panel of the card, readers have only a hint that this might be a wedding invitation, based on the floral graphic and the silhouette (Figure 1.2a), but opening the card, readers find a visual puzzle, with the couple hidden in a mélange of cartoon characters, animals, and city structures (Figure 1.2b). When the card is fully opened, one four-panel side includes text that most closely resembles an invitation, with the reader being told—in English, Korean, and Japanese—that a "power-house duo will emerge" from an event in December 2010 (Figure 1.2c). Obligatory moves are included, such as the date, time, and place, and some suggestion of a wedding (entirely a visual suggestion, in this case); still, very little about this invitation is traditional, with its bright colors, its extensive code-mixing, and its playful text. While wedding invitations often bend tradition in small ways in order to individual-ize their invitations, by violating multiple conventions, the invitation in Figure 1.2 (a–c) is an example of more extreme innovation. Never-theless, although it may not be immediately recognizable as a wed-ding invitation, it still manages to carry out the primary social action of inviting friends and family to a wedding, so it still makes sense to classify it within the wedding invitation genre.

The examples in Figures 1.1 and 1.2 (a–c) are in many ways the most common types of innovations we might encounter—subtle (or not-so-subtle) experimentations with a genre's textual appearance. But if we consider genres to be social actions and genre knowledge to encompass an understanding of how a genre is typically carried out, then we should also consider how users might depart from non-textual expectations. In other words, an innovative instance of a genre doesn't necessarily need to look different in its textual instantiation—the inno-vation may occur behind the scenes, so to speak, and it may eventually lead to the creation of a new genre. Consider, for example, the case of self-published ebooks, a relatively new phenomenon. As opposed to print books, ebooks are digitally born and distributed, but they are also distinct in the processes through which they are produced. In a digital ethnography of self-published ebooks in the online poker community, Laquintano (2010) explains that the formal conventions

Figure 1.2a. Wedding Invitation Front

Where Have Pat And Youngju Gone?
パットとヨンジュはどこでしょう
팻과 영주는 어디에 있을까요?

Figure 1.2b. Wedding Invitation Puzzle

of these books are not themselves unusual, bearing some resemblance to mathematics textbooks, but the practices for textual production are unique. The writing process integrates reader feedback from the beginning, as authors solicit reader opinions about style and content, and readers even contribute to text editing. As Laquintano describes it, this process results in a kind of sustained, distributed authorship that blurs the roles of writer, readers, and publisher. While the genre itself may still be considered an innovative variety of certain paper-based texts,

Figure 1.2c. Wedding Invitation Inside Panel

Wedding invitation used with permission.

its growing use and prevalence are likely leading it to quickly gain status as its own genre. Innovation, after all, requires newness and an element of surprise and therefore cannot be repeated too many times before it morphs into convention.

The types of genre innovations described so far demonstrate obvious departures from convention, but innovation is not always characterized by this kind of difference. In some cases, as Pennycook (2007) demonstrates, innovation may arise from adherence to convention. Looking specifically at hip-hop, sampling, and re-mixing, or, in the words of a hip-hop artist, "creating with found objects" (Pennycook, 2007, p. 580), Pennycook suggests that language creativity and play is at times the result of sameness—through recontextualization and repetition—as much as it is the result of difference. He identifies copying, parodying, and mimicking as examples of "sameness that create difference: they differ from the original and simultaneously change the original through recontextualization" (p. 587). The use of parody and imitation as innovation, even subversion, is also described by Canagarajah (2006b) as he shares how academic scholars at the geopolitical periphery may use dominant conventions ironically, essentially "playing the game" while poking fun of the rules. An interest in parody is not new to genre theory, having been explored in early work by Swales (1993) and briefly by Devitt (2004). By mimicking and often exaggerating convention, parodies draw attention to features of genres—most important, the social contexts, goals, and outcomes of them—and in doing so, carry out functions not intended by the original genre. In other words, the innovation occurs at the level of rhetorical action and perhaps procedural practice.

This section began by posing genre knowledge as one possible framework for understanding genre innovation, and I've used that framework here to consider several examples of common innovative approaches to genre. The framework is not a perfect fit, but it has potential for including innovations that go beyond the visible text features that readers may easily notice. If what writers *know* about a genre encompasses the form, rhetorical strategies, procedural practices, and ideational content (and the inter-connections of these dimensions), they may well draw on these same knowledge dimensions when seeking to bend—or avoid bending—conventions, resulting in texts that depart from or conform to others' expectations. Furthermore, it may be the case that the rich, multi-layered genre knowledge of experts better enables effective innovation, or that different genres draw on different aspects of genre knowledge for effective innovation. Research has not yet examined these questions, but they are certainly worthy of more consideration.

A Case for Studying Genre Innovation

So far this chapter has laid the foundation for an argument for studying genre innovation by considering how innovation relates to convention and by attempting to define and illustrate innovation as it relates to genre theory. I have hinted at, but skirted somewhat around, the question of why an extended exploration of genre innovation is worthy of study. Given that much interest in genre is grounded in the goal of developing genre awareness for novices, including an awareness of convention, why attend to the less common instances of genres that are so often associated with expert users? Is such an exploration a worthwhile endeavor for those interested in supporting writers who are still developing genre familiarity?

First, we know relatively little about genre innovation from a theoretical perspective, but understanding this creative and dynamic aspect of genre can contribute to our theories of genre. Given the fundamental importance of genre in communication, such a goal is in itself worthwhile. Devitt (2004) poses several questions for future research to take on, such as understanding better when the use or non-use of particular genre features is noticed, and how genres sustain both conventions and variations. Less explicitly, discussions of innovation are also tied up with reception and, therefore, power. A focus on genre innovation, then, has the potential to develop our understanding of how power acts on genres and their writers, and how writers may work within and challenge systems of power through genres. Developing a more sophisticated understanding of this aspect of genre has important implications for genre learners, who are generally positioned in less powerful positions. And if, as Kress (1999) and Hyland (2000) have argued, genres are indices of their social worlds, understanding the possibilities for genre innovation is just important as understanding genre conventions; both processes can give us insight into the social worlds that surround them.

A study of innovation and genre also seems particularly relevant at this historical point in time. As Blommaert (2010) notes in *The Sociolinguistics of Globalization*, our theories of discourse and language need to play catch-up to account for the new explosion of diversity and mobility that characterize the 21st century. While Blommaert focuses primarily on public discourses, such diversity and mobility is also a fact of life in today's academic world, in which scholars study, conduct research, collaborate, and disseminate ideas all over the world—and increasingly in one language. Indeed, as monolingual English speakers become the minority in this global community of scholars, we may fast be approaching what Malcolm Gladwell (2000) refers to as a "tipping point": "that one dramatic moment in an epidemic when everything can change all at once" (2000, p. 9). The implications of diversity, mobility, and global communication on the genres of academic writing have yet to be explored. But more attempts at and opportunities for innovation within genres seem likely, if not inevitable, making innovation an increasingly relevant part of genre and discourse theory.

New processes of globalization act locally as well. Increased migration, for example, has led to greater linguistic diversity within the classrooms of many Anglophone countries, including Australia, Canada, the U.K., and the U.S. In the United States, universities and colleges are experiencing diversity in new ways, forcing writing studies scholars and practitioners to come to terms with pedagogical approaches and disciplinary lenses that now at times seem somewhat anachronistic. While calls for new approaches and even paradigms are currently gaining more visibility in this context, they have tended to focus almost solely on strategies and opportunities for student innovation while generally overlooking the question of how such innovations are responded to by peers, teachers, and other gatekeepers. Knowing more about the constraints and opportunities for innovation that act on student writers, even in diverse educational contexts, can have important implications for writing instruction.

As genre conventions reflect and reinforce particular values and ideologies, playing with or flouting those conventions also offers the opportunity to challenge conventional ways of knowing. Therefore, a study of genre innovation can also inform our understanding of the dynamics of knowledge production, both within and across disciplines. Innovative or alternative approaches to knowledge production may, when received positively, have a rippling effect on genres, so that a research method or epistemic style that was at one point viewed as risky or cutting edge may at a later point be considered mainstream. As diverse groups of students and scholars enact traditional genres, we may find a wider range of approaches to knowledge production. Research in academic settings can inform our understanding of when and why certain innovations are embraced while others are soundly rejected or simply ignored.

Finally, exploring innovation in genres may have important implications for teaching writing to both monolingual and multilingual learners. If a goal of using genres is to develop ownership over them, including the ability to appropriate and manipulate them for one's own purposes (Bhatia, 2004), innovation could play a valuable role in the learning process. New work in language and creativity suggests that encouraging language play—which might include genre play— can have valuable benefits for learning (Pomerantz & Bell, 2007; see also Chapter 5), but much more research in this area is still needed.

While in many ways this book will take a theoretical approach to understanding genre innovation, it is at the same time motivated by the practical matters of learning and using academic genres. I will therefore take up several questions that are both theoretically and pedagogically motivated. Primarily, this book considers when and why intentional or unintentional departures from generic norms are embraced or rejected by dominant readers. Are opportunities for innovation limited to experts, or can the texts of learners and novices also be viewed as innovative? In probing these questions, I will explore several related issues: What kinds of innovations are possible in different genres and communities, or by authors of different status levels? What constraints act to deter innovation? Are there still opportunities for innovation/ variation in high-stakes, heavily regulated genres? For whom? How does innovation/deviation operate in globalized contexts? How does the ability to innovate relate to genre knowledge development? To what extent might "genre play" facilitate genre learning?

Chapter 2

A Theoretical and Methodological Toolkit

While current genre theory provides a starting point for an in-depth exploration of genre innovation, further study can be enriched by related areas of scholarship that have studied innovation more directly. In this chapter, I review several lines of such inquiry, including the study of innovation, creativity, and identity, with the goal of identifying conceptual and methodological tools that have practical value for the study of genre innovation in academic writing. Following a discussion of relevant research, I offer a summary and application of the key principles derived from this research, and then finally turn to possible methodologies for studying genre innovation.

Theories of Innovation

Although my ultimate aim is to better understand innovation within and through academic writing, much insight can be gained by looking more broadly at research in discourse and language studies that has examined intentional departures from expectations. In this section, I consider relevant work from several areas, including rhetoric and composition, sociolinguistics, and applied linguistics.

Alternative Discourses

Since the 1990s, there has been a growing interest in innovation within U.S.-based Composition Studies, a field heavily focused on writing instruction for U.S. undergraduates. This work often falls under the rubric of "alternative discourses," "hybridity," or "codemeshing" (see, for example, Schroeder, Fox, & Bizzell, 2002, and Young & Martinez, 2011). Thaiss and Zawacki (2006) have attempted to describe the different strategies for challenging dominant discourses (outlined previously in Chapter 1) by drawing primarily on interview and survey data, but most scholarship in this area is more theoretical than empirical. One of the primary goals of this work has been to argue for the acceptance of hybridized or alternative discourses within the academy as a means of giving voice to students or scholars who have been traditionally marginalized. Alternatives here are situated specifically in opposition to dominant discourses, which are characterized not just by their preference for a particular language variety (typically "standard English") or by certain genres but also by the worldview that they adopt (Bizzell, 2002). So, on the one hand, this work argues for finding a place for marginalized voices, and, on the other hand, it considers the potential that alternative discourses have to disrupt dominant worldviews; in Bizzell's words, innovations "allow their practitioners to do intellectual work in ways they could not if confined to traditional academic discourse" (p. 3). Nevertheless, possibilities for alternative discourses are always socially situated, and judgments of both how "alternative" a discourse is and how suitable it is are tied to dominant ideologies and social conditions (Mao, 2002). Matsuda (2002), therefore, has described alternative discourses as "marked forms of discourse used within a particular site of discourse practices and in a certain sociohistorical context" (p. 192). This emphasis on context is essential to understanding how innovation may function within genre, a form of discourse that is inherently bound to social context.

Flouting and the Cooperative Principle

Within the field of pragmatics, departures from communication norms are often characterized as *flouts*, following Grice's (1975, 1989) concept of the Cooperative Principle. According to this principle, participants in a conversation should "make [their] conversational contribution such as is required, at the stage at which it occurs, by the accepted purpose or direction of the talk exchange in which [they] are engaged" (Grice, 1989, p. 26). Grice further outlined four sub-principles, or maxims, to guide such participation in terms of *quantity* (be informative), *quality* (be truthful), *relation* (be relevant), and *manner* (be perspicuous or clear). Importantly, Grice acknowledged that participants may fail to fulfill one or more maxims for various reasons, including the speaker's decision to *flout*, or exploit, the maxim. This notion of flouting calls to mind the purposeful decision of writers to exploit, bend, or break genre conventions.

Greenall (2009) offers one of the very few theoretical explorations of flouting, characterizing flouts as "out-of-frame occurrences" that, because of their unexpectedness, attract attention and result in "increased interpretational activity" (p. 2296)—in other words, flouts engage their interlocutors as they consider the reasons for and functions of the departure. In building a theory of flouting, Greenall also turns to Alfred Schutz's concept of *thematic relevance* (Schutz & Luckmann, 1973), which describes humans' desire to turn to unusual objects, events, or actions when making sense of the world. What Schutz terms *imposed thematic relevances* arise when interlocutors find an unusual or unexpected element within a familiar frame—a description that seems also to describe the kinds of generic innovations we considered in Chapter 1. Greenall finds imposed thematic relevances to encompass flouting of maxims:

> It is in this sense that maxim breach becomes a *deviation*, and as long as this breach/deviation is "fresh" (i.e., has not yet become conventionalized or "generalized"…), a non-observance or flout will, as a matter of principle, end up in one of more of the categories "unusual," or "unfamiliar," or "unexpected." (p. 2300)

Greenall goes on to note that, in most cases, texts with flouts or non-observances follow convention more than they depart from it, except in the case of humorous texts or advertising. This tendency is not surprising; as we saw in Chapter 1, violating too many conventions would put the recognizability of the genre at risk.

Greenall outlines three types of detectable flouts, including *opting out* (which occurs when speakers or writers explicitly announce to their interlocutors that they will violate a convention—as in the case of a phrase like *This might not be relevant, but…*; *flagrant non-observance* (deliberate deviations that are not explicitly called out), and *infringement* (unintentional deviations caused by a lack of understanding of the conventions or the linguistic code, or perhaps by a situational factors such as anxiety or high emotion). One final aspect of Greenall's (2009) discussion of flouting that holds particular value for genre innovation is her discussion of reasons for departing from convention. These include: (1) to convey a particular idea or meaning or (2) to portray the speaker (or writer) in a particular way. This theoretical fleshing out of the notion of maxims valuably turns our attention to the functions, reasons for, and possible effects of deviations from perceived norms and thus has potential use in understanding innovation to genres.

Discourse Disruptions

An interest in the reception of departures from dominant discourse conventions has also been taken up in applied linguistics. One of the most notable works in this area is Guy Cook's *Discourse and Literature* (1994). The book focuses on literary language, but it nonetheless offers useful frameworks for understanding innovation in written academic genres. Drawing heavily on *schema theory* (related to the notion of frames described in Chapter 1), Cook's exploration of language play specifically considers readers' reactions to literary texts in terms of "discourse disruptions." Texts that deviate significantly from (or *disrupt*) schematic expectations are characterized by Cook as "schema refreshing" discourse; texts that generally adhere to norms might be characterized as "schema reinforcing" or "schema preserving." Cook argues that the main function of schema refreshing discourses "is to effect a change in the schemata of their readers" (p. 191). This change may be manifested in pleasure, entertainment, even anger—in essence, it is the reader's response to or uptake of a text. If a discourse departs too drastically from expectation, it may be rejected; such judgments are always reader-dependent, sensitive to each individual's expectations and tolerance for departures. Widdowson (2008) takes a similar perspective, situating creative acts theoretically as perlocutionary effects brought about by a disruption of expectations.

For the study of genre and innovation, one particularly useful aspect of Cook's (1994) framework is the delineation of different types of schemata and, therefore, different types of schematic deviations. Texts can follow or break norms for world schemata (e.g., general knowledge), text schemata (e.g., structure), or language schemata (e.g., grammar). Cook argues that deviations to the higher-level world schemata are necessary for a text to be schema refreshing, and he acknowledges that text and language schemata may in fact alter world schemata. On this point, we find important connections with genre theory, which contends that the structural and linguistic choices of texts both reflect and reinforce particular values (i.e., world schemata) (e.g., Berkenkotter & Huckin, 1995; Kamberelis, 1995); therefore, we might consider deviations in these formal areas to be reflections of epistemological or ideological alternatives, much in line with Bizzell's (2002) argument that alternative discourses (or discursive manifestations) have the potential to offer alternative worldviews.

Language Games and Language Play

These frameworks for alternative, marked, non-observant, or disruptive discourses discuss departures in a relatively broad sense, but another noteworthy line of scholarship considers very specific kinds of alternatives—namely those predicated on the notion of play. Relating language use to play or games is not new; in language and writing studies, references are frequently made to Wittgenstein's (1968) metaphor of language games, Saussure's (1983) comparison of language to chess, and Bakhtin's (1963/1968) analogy of language as a carnival. The game metaphor, importantly, assumes the existence of rules or guidelines and player roles, a principle that similarly undergirds much rhetorical genre theory. Game play, in other words, doesn't happen in a completely unstructured way but rather draws on some shared assumptions and purposes. In her case studies of advanced academic writers, Casanave (2002) adopts a game metaphor rooted primarily in Ortner's (1996) game theory, which emphasizes the role of power within games. Such a perspective, Casanave (2002) argues, can help to show "how people in concrete settings, including academic ones, contest for power, find themselves included and excluded, and use intentionality and agency to skillfully and strategically play and 'stretch' (i.e., change) the game" (p. 18).

In her well-known work on uptake, Anne Freadman (1987) applies the game analogy directly to genres, and she counters the assumption that production of a genre text is simply an application of a set of rigid rules. Rather, she specifies, that the "rules" are "*rules for play*" (p. 95, emphasis in original):

> Using a text is primarily a matter of understanding its genre and the way it plays it—recognising it, certainly, but also reading its tactics, its strategies, and its ceremonial place. Learning to write, equally, is learning to appropriate and occupy a place in relation to other texts, learning to ensure that the other chap will play the appropriate game with you, and learning to secure a useful uptake: the rules for playing, the rules of play, and the tricks of the trade. (pp. 121–122)

The *game*, then, is characterized by a ceremonial place, the interplay or dialogue with another (or others), and the strategies and tactics implemented by the players.

A focus on language play—as opposed to language *games*—has been taken up by several applied linguists in the past decade as well. In general, this work focuses less on the existence of the larger conventions or frames within which play operates and more on the kinds of play in which language users engage and the effects of such play on (usually oral) interactions and language learning. Carter (2004), Cook (2000), and Crystal (1998), for example, have looked at the various ways in which speakers manipulate language through rhymes, puns, repetition, hyperbole, and other literary techniques. One interesting finding of this work has been the pervasiveness of play in everyday language. In other words, unexpected playful and creative uses of language are actually quite common, especially among friends and family engaging in intimate (versus transactional) conversation. Given Carter's (2004) finding that occurrences of play vary by interaction type, we might similarly expect that manipulations of genre conventions are dependent on the genre function and community of users. More research is needed in this area, but this scholarship into language and play offers a useful starting point.

The Study of Creativity

Much of the work I have reviewed so far either tacitly or directly references creativity as one possible aspect of innovation. Not all innovations might be considered creative, but, in most cases, creative texts or acts are considered innovative. Given the association of creativity with newness and unexpected departures, then, it is worth examining this concept in more depth. In this section, I review ways in which creativity has been defined, theorized, and studied within the fields of Creativity Studies, Applied Linguistics, World Englishes, and Discourse Studies.

Creativity Research

Creativity Studies has indeed become a growing area of interdisciplinary research, of interest to both the general public (evidenced in several popular books on the topic) and to those studying areas as diverse as advertising, workplace organizations, intelligence, education, fine arts, and scientific discovery.

Within this field, definitions of and theoretical approaches to creativity abound (Kozbelt, Beghetto, & Runco, 2010; Sawyer, 2012), though most share the view that creativity is characterized by originality (often described as novelty) and usefulness (often described as appropriateness, value, or utility) (Mayer, 1999; cf. Pope, 2005). Conceptions of creativity are also socially and historically bounded, so that something that may be considered creative in one space and time is not necessarily deemed creative in a different space and time (Lubart, 2010; Sawyer, 2012). Early work on creativity within psychology often aimed to identify measurable characteristics of creative thinking, examining correlations between personality traits or intelligence with creativity. Though much of this work has since been abandoned, some contemporary research still looks specifically at "creative people," and some of these findings seem to have implications for a study of genre and innovation. Gardner (1993), for instance, proposed that creative individuals often come from the margins of society rather than the center; this argument would suggest that bringing an "outsider's perspective" could play an important role in being *perceived* as creative by people in the center—a suggestion that would certainly have implications for transnational writing settings. Research has also found associations between creativity and expertise, or experience in and mastery of a specific knowledge domain. The popular image of someone who effortlessly and spontaneously produces a game-changing work of art or scientific discovery is what Sawyer (2012) calls a *creativity myth*. Products deemed creative or path-breaking are instead much more likely to be the result of formal training, conscious thought, sustained hard work, and high productivity.

Many investigations of creativity—and indeed references to creativity within writing and language scholarship—assume it to be a property of a person, product, or idea. Such an assumption, it follows, views creativity as an objective quality: a product is or is not creative, regardless of the circumstances under which it is viewed, read, and/or judged. Yet a theory of creativity that takes reception into account would seem more useful to the study of written genres, and it is here that sociocultural approaches to creativity have much to offer. In this school of thought, "a product is creative when experts in the domain agree it is creative" (Amabile, 1982, p. 1001). A sociocultural orientation puts reception front and center and emphasizes the important criterion of appropriateness; judgments of creativity can only be assigned when something is considered to be both novel and appropriate. Sawyer (2012) offers the example of a creative piece of music, such as a sonata. In order for the piece to be perceived as a sonata, it must work within certain conventions of that kind of music. If it departs too far from these conventions, it may no longer be considered a sonata; if it doesn't depart very far at all (i.e., if it is not sufficiently novel), it may not be considered creative. Judgments of a product as appropriate are obviously tied to sociohistoric contexts, and though creativity theory tends not to highlight the power structures of such contexts, power is most certainly at play.

One framework for understanding perceptions of creativity is put forth by the psychologist Mihaly Csikszentmihalyi, who is also known for his work on the concept of flow. Csikszentmihalyi's (1996, 1999) sociocultural model of creativity consists of three interacting components: *the person* who serves as the source of the innovation; *the field*, defined specifically as the social networks or gatekeepers who initially evaluate the product's novelty and appropriateness; and *the domain*, made up of the larger system for conventions and common practices. It is the interaction among these components that results in a judgment of creativity. More specifically, the innovator creates a product or idea, usually working within the repertoire of available norms, expectations, and conventions that circulate within the domain. The field judges the product—if it is considered by them to be creative or innovative, it enters the domain, adding to the existing resources and norms. If these gatekeepers deem the product to be unsuccessful, it is rejected and does not enter the domain. Importantly, research shows that experts (who serve as gatekeepers) tend to agree largely on judgments of creativity, much more so than novices or generalists (Sawyer, 2012), demonstrating that systems of cultural reproduction are at play. This systems-based framework offers great heuristic potential for understanding reception and judgments of creativity, though it has been perhaps somewhat under-utilized in creativity research because of its complexity and qualitative nature. Pope (2005) notes that Csikszentmihalyi's framework also tends to downplay the important collaborative nature of creativity, despite the attention that it gives to the interaction of social elements. For writing studies, nevertheless, this systems-based approach has strong potential for understanding how written products may be evaluated as creative or, more broadly, innovative within particular social contexts.

Language and Creativity

Creativity research has recently been picked up in the field of Applied Linguistics as well. Currently, the most popular strand works within what Jones (2010) calls the "language and creativity" paradigm. Some examples of work in this area include the research by Crystal (1998),

Cook (2000), and Carter (2004) discussed previously, as well as several studies in the volume *Creativity in Language and Literature* (Swann, Pope, & Carter, 2011). Jones characterizes these approaches as focusing primarily on language products, much in the spirit of a stylistics analysis, while giving short shrift to the processes and contexts of creativity. Indeed, Carter (2007) himself echoes this sentiment to some extent, calling for language and creativity research to pay more attention to product reception and to judgments of creativity, invoking the sociocultural approach previously discussed. Additional work of note in language and creativity includes Maybin and Swann's (2007) framework for analyzing creative language along three integrated dimensions: textual, contextual, and critical. The goal of such a framework is to look beyond textual dimensions of play, addressing some of the concerns that Carter expresses. Finally, a study of language play in the foreign language classroom suggests that play—or creative uses of language—may play a role in language learning (Pomerantz & Bell, 2007).

In contrast to the language and creativity paradigm, Jones (2010) advocates for a "discourse and creativity" paradigm, which examines non-literary discourse to explore how language might be used strategically in specific social settings to effect change. This approach, he argues, takes a broader social perspective, has a particular interest in power relations, and considers the functions or outcomes of creative uses of language. Though coming from slightly different approaches, however, both Carter (2007) and Jones (2010) agree that robust explorations of creativity and language/discourse must take social context and reception seriously and therefore demand ethnographic research approaches in addition to text-based analysis. Some integration of these two approaches may be particularly useful for studying creativity in genre.

Creativity and World Englishes

One area of applied language study that has long been attuned to issues of innovation and creativity, particularly in relation to the global use and spread of English, is the field known as World Englishes (WE). In his early work, *The Alchemy of English*, Braj Kachru (1986) described four major functions that English plays in the postcolonial context of

South Asia: instrumental, regulative, interpersonal, and innovative (also referred to as the creative or imaginative function). The innovative function in WE generally refers to the creative "nativization" of English in literature or advertising—the ways in which writers adopt and adapt English to express local sensibilities. Lexical innovations might include, for example, Tamil words that enter British English or hybridized expressions that mix two languages (e.g., *tiffin carrier* to describe the person who delivers lunches in tins in India) (Kachru, 1986). These innovations are not flouts or discourse disruptions in the same sense that we have previously discussed because they are used to establish new local norms rather than to challenge expectations.

In his discussion of nativizations in English, Bamgboṣe (1998) proposes to differentiate between innovation (at the lexical, pragmatic, or creative levels) and error, describing the former as an acceptable variant and the latter as a mistake. When it becomes difficult to distinguish the two, Bamgboṣe suggests looking to factors internal to the English variety, specifically: "How many people use the innovation? How widely dispersed is it? Who uses it? Where is the usage sanctioned? What is the attitude of users and non-users to it?" (p. 3). In the end, he argues that codification of non-native Englishes, based on internal rather than external norms, is a crucial step to granting legitimacy to innovations. Though Bamgboṣe's interest is in local, more than transnational, contexts, this discussion of innovation and error suggests several important factors that might influence judgments of innovation by multilingual writers in international English-using contexts, including the uses, users, and setting.

In addition to innovation, WE has also taken interest in creativity, with bilinguals' creativity having been the subject of inquiry from the 1980s to present. Bilinguals' creativity is defined by Kachru (1985) as "those creative linguistic processes which are the result of competence in two or more languages" (p. 20) and involve the manipulation and appropriation of English structures and functions within a new ecology (Bhatt, 2001). Such processes may be motivated, as well, by desired stylistic effects or expressions of identity (Kachru, 1985). While the concept of bilinguals' creativity may seem quite general with regards to language use, much WE scholarship in this area has explored it in terms of literary language (e.g., Baker & Eggington, 1999;

Tawake, 2003). In contrast, almost no research has looked at bilingual creativity in academic or professional texts, and, further, instances of creativity studied in this area have tended to focus on sentence-level lexical or grammatical innovations rather than on broader discursive innovations (Yajun & Chenggang, 2006; cf. Kachru, 1997; You, 2011).

More recently, a 2010 issue of *World Englishes* was devoted to creativity in WE, and here we find a more expansive approach to the subject. In particular, Jones (2010) argues for an approach to creativity that, rather than focusing solely on text, looks at "the kinds of strategies bilingual writers use to overcome inevitable problems of cultural and linguistic translatability of their work" (p. 470). Seen this way, creativity is not merely the use of linguistic strategies like word play, hyperbole, or code-mixing, but can instead be thought of as a way of responding to or acting within a situation. Jones' goal for such research is far-reaching: "When we speak of 'creativity' from this perspective," he argues, "we are not just talking about changing language in some clever or inventive way—we are talking about changing the world" (p. 473).

Creativity and Discourse in the 21ˢᵗ Century

Understanding how language (not specifically English) works in today's globalized society has also been a focus of those interested in discourse and globalization, evidenced by several book-length treatments of the topic (e.g., Blommaert, 2010; Fairclough, 2006; Pennycook, 2010, 2012). As Blommaert (2010) aptly notes, today's symbolic market place is transnational with flexible boundaries, and theories of discourse need to account for its *"mobile* resources, *mobile* speakers and *mobile* markets" (p. 29, emphasis in original). In his work, Blommaert offers several theoretical concepts that can inform an understanding of how innovation plays out within such an environment.

To account for the highly mobile nature of today's discourse, Blommaert (2005) develops a concept that he terms "orders of indexicality"—a jargon-ridden term, to be sure, but one that is extremely productive for studying genre innovation. Blommaert defines orders of indexicality, an expression that nods to Foucault's (1982) "orders of discourse," as "reproduced, stratified meanings often called 'norms' or 'rules' of language" (p. 73). When we orient toward particular orders of indexicality (or "norms"), we reproduce them while displaying our affiliation with them. By using the term *order*, Blommaert highlights the hierarchical nature of indexical meanings—some indexicalities are granted legitimacy and prestige while others may be stigmatized. Further, not all people have access to all indexicalities or to the forms used within them.

Important shifts occur when a writer orients toward the meaning-making symbols and norms of one space, but the text is then taken up in another, where different norms hold sway. Such shifts are common in transnational writing in which a text is produced in one locality (whether physical or not) and then received within a different locality. In these situations, the transported text may not be read or heard in the way the author had hoped; in other words, it may fail to index the intended meaning or it may carry out unintended functions because meaning is not inherent to a text but is instead assigned locally. Relating these kinds of shifts to innovation, Blommaert (2005) notes that the movement of texts across environments may also lead to "shifts in judgements of creativity . . . and thus also the capacity to be perceived as creative" (p. 106). One simple example of this mobility problem might be found in the popular Japan Railways (JR) advertisement campaign that relies on the popular slogan: *train + ing = traing*, or alternatively just TRAiNG™. While the slogan has endured for many years, implying its success, foreigners I knew when living in Japan often expressed confusion about the meaning and were perplexed about why it was successful—some were even bothered by its manipulation (or "faulty" use) of English. But, as Blommaert's work shows, the ad was not intended for foreigners; it was meant to function *locally* and be interpreted through local orders of indexicality. Blommaert's work, like others we have discussed in this chapter, situates judgment or reception as a key to innovation, leaving writers in a highly mobile environment with the hard work of imagining the potential re-locations of their texts and the receptions of those texts based on the newly assigned meanings. Further, to understand perceptions of innovation, we need to understand the different environments in which a text and its author(s) might be produced and received, somewhat complicating the systems-based model of creativity described earlier.

Blommaert's (2005) new theory of discourse also brings power and access to the analytic table, urging us to look at the value and mobility of the meaning-making resources to which writers have access. Put simply, some resources are more readily mobile than others. Those that are more constrained in their mobility may lack market value when they move from local to global contexts—they are, in Blommaert's words, "structurally disenfranchised" (p. 95). Blommaert's reminders of the inequities involved in transnational communication offer a counterpoint to Devitt's (2004, 2011) and Schryer's (2011) more optimistic representations of genres as choice. Instead, he argues quite specifically that while "people do indeed creatively select forms of discourse...there is a limit to choice and freedom" (Bloomaert, 2005, p. 99). This work suggests, then, that any exploration of genre and innovation in transnational contexts must consider a relatively complex web of issues, such as an author's intentions, the resources to which an author has or does not have access, any shifts that take place between a text's production and reception, the potential for the text to carry its meanings and functions with it when re-located, the functions or meanings assigned to the text upon reception, and the power structures that characterize the contexts of production and reception.

Identity, Ethos, and Legitimacy

Departures from generic norms and expectations—whether instances of play, creativity, or resistance—tend to draw attention to a text's producer, giving importance to issues of authorial identity. Relationships between language and identity are complex, and a thorough discussion of these relationships is beyond the scope of my discussion here, but at least some aspects of authorial identity need to be considered in order to explore genre innovation.

First, the assertion of individuality may be one reason for an author's decision to depart from generic norms, just as Greenall (2009) posits it to be a reason for flouting more generally. By recombining or appropriating the voices of others in our own ways (Bakhtin, 1986), we take ownership over our writing and create an "imprint of individuality" (Bakhtin, 1986, p. 75). This assertion of identity is generally considered to be performative and contingent rather than stable or unitary.

Further, different discourses make available different resources upon which authors can draw to project particular identities (Hyland, 2010). In other words, identities occur within, rather than apart from, discourses.

Individual projections of identity are also often referred to as voice, which is another useful, if at times ambiguous, notion for understanding the reception of genre innovation. Contemporary research has often invoked a sociocultural definition of voice, in which voice is constructed *by readers* as they interact with a text (e.g., Matsuda, 2001; Prior, 2001). This view widens the lens of author identity to consider not just the choices that an author makes within a discursive system but also the ways in which those choices construct the author for others. Taking a macro, contextualized view, this line of research emphasizes the dialogic nature of identity and the critical role that readers play in its construction (Matsuda, 2015; Tardy, 2012a, in press). Relying on textual and contextual features, readers make note of adherence to and departure from convention to form certain impressions of authors, including their experience, disciplinary knowledge, and perhaps even personality or gender (Matsuda & Tardy, 2007).

Discussions of identity and voice are often linked closely to *ethos*, or author credibility, as well. Studies of academic genres have identified numerous strategies that authors use to establish credibility, such as the use of particular rhetorical moves, hedges or boosters, and discipline-specific jargon (see, for example, Hyland, 2000). *Ethos* is relevant to genre innovation because it conditions, at least in part, readers' judgments of whether the author has the right to bend a genre. Cherry (1998) provides a thorough discussion of *ethos*, including Aristotle's original use of the term. For Aristotle, *ethos* encompassed three related aspects of author self-representation: the portrayal of oneself as having good moral (and intellectual) character, practical wisdom, and a concern for audience (Cherry, 1998). It is through these characteristics that a writer may gain readers' trust and respect; by extension, it seems that establishing *ethos* would also allow a writer to depart from convention with the approval of readers. *Ethos* is difficult to separate from other aspects of author self-representation, such as identity or voice, as the choices that an author makes in constructing an identity are very often wrapped up in the desire to establish *ethos*. Further, the voice(s) or identity/identities that a reader ascribes to an author may establish the author as credible, good willed, or even disrespectful of the audience, thereby contributing to the writer's *ethos*.

An additional model for understanding a writer's right to bend generic convention can be found in Bourdieu's economic metaphor of the linguistic market. Though limited in its acknowledgement of individual agency, Bourdieu's work does offer a useful starting point for linking readers and writers within a social context explicitly marked by power structures. For Bourdieu (1991), an utterance cannot be recognized as authoritative, or granted social power, unless it satisfies three "ritual conditions" (p. 113): It must be produced by a legitimate authority, it must be produced within a legitimate situation, and it must be produced in legitimate forms. Focusing on the first of these three conditions leads us to the question of who can be considered a "legitimate authority"? Within Bourdieu's model, legitimacy for speakers (or writers) is granted through the accumulation of linguistic, symbolic, or cultural capital. It is not surprising that many examples of innovation in academic writing come from authors who have already established their linguistic and disciplinary competence and who hold relatively high status within their field. These writers can exchange their accumulated capital for the right to deviate from dominant norms because they benefit from what Bourdieu calls a profit of distinction. That is, they have access to scarce linguistic competences (language varieties, genres, discourses) that hold social power, and the relative scarcity of these competencies makes them more valuable or profitable. But "legitimate" writers likely also bring with them other forms of accumulated capital, such as professional and/or cultural capital. Even names or academic titles may grant legitimacy because of their symbolic scarcity.

What emerges from this complicated web of authorial identity is something of a vicious cycle marked by power and access: Experienced authors gain access to the resources that allow them to produce legitimate language in legitimate forms and situations; in doing so, they accumulate symbolic capital; their capital then allows them to exploit the system and perhaps stray from norms in ways that those with less capital cannot; through their distinctive uses of language they may accumulate further legitimacy and power within the market.

Finally, discussions of authors and their self-representation and construction often bring to mind writing **style**, a term I've not yet used but have skirted around. Style can be linked to individuals, genres, or discourses, or simultaneously to all three; style may also be linked to creativity, particularly in studies of literary language. I will limit my use of the term here for two reasons. First, the term is too broad to be of particular theoretical use in understanding innovation; second, and more importantly, I'd like to avoid conflating style with innovation. Certainly some stylistic choices can be innovative, as we saw in Chapter 1, but style is not always innovative nor is all innovation stylistic in nature. Therefore, I will consider style as one potential source of innovation but also acknowledge that it is not always associated with individuals nor is it necessarily innovative.

Summary of Conceptual Tools

So far we have considered several conceptual tools that can contribute to an understanding of genre and innovation. Before moving on to look at research of innovation in academic settings, it may be useful to pause here to synthesize some of the elements of genre innovation that we can derive from the discussion in Chapters 1 and 2, focusing on four major areas.

Types of Innovations

Generally, the most obvious types of innovation are those that are textual in nature, such as hybridized genres or linguistic codes, unexpected alterations to typical generic move structures or visual elements, or playful or literary manipulations of language. But research suggests that disruptions or innovations to discourse can operate on multiple levels, and various models have been offered to investigate these levels. We might, for example, consider innovation at the level of language (e.g., lexico-grammar), text (e.g., structure), or world (e.g., general knowledge) schemata, following Cook (1994), or we could employ a framework of genre knowledge, which posits that genre users draw on knowledge of form, rhetoric, subject-matter content, procedures, and practices. Both of these frameworks emphasize that innovations include visible departures to expected forms but also extend to larger knowledge domains.

Some scholarship (e.g., Cook, 1994) argues that the most disruptive or highly innovative texts might be those that depart from expectations beyond language form—for example, those that challenge our world schemas—providing additional rationale for looking beyond the most obviously marked departures. At the same time, deviations to form, or rhetorical strategies, may also challenge world schemas as they often index larger worldviews or epistemologies. Research also suggests that a study of innovation needs to consider *sameness* in texts as well as *difference,* as texts may re-use or re-appropriate genre conventions in ways that bend norms and expectations.

Reasons for Innovating

Genre innovations, at any level of discourse, may be the result of different actions or motivations by writers. While some norm-departures may be the result of a writer's lack of knowledge or experience with a genre, language, or setting (what Greenall [2009] calls *infringement*), others may be very purposefully integrated. This distinction is important because, while innovations are generally considered intentional, the intent of the writer is not always evident to text readers. Decisions to depart from convention may be motivated by a writer's desire to portray him- or herself in a particular way or to express ideas or content in a particular way; the former choices are linked to issues of identity while the latter may be related to an interest in bringing in marginalized voices or new ways of knowledge construction. In Chapter 3, I explore in much more detail the various reasons that writers might attempt to innovate.

Frames and Genre Knowledge

Many discussions of discourse norm-departures rely on metaphors of frames, schemata, or games, all of which are also apt metaphors for genres. Extending the frame metaphor to prototype theory, we might see innovative genre-texts as departing from prototypes in some ways but still sharing enough "family resemblances" to be granted genre membership and legitimacy. Frame metaphors also offer useful ways to understand the potential for innovation within genre, because they suggest that "play" with or "non-observance" of conventions must still occur within the available, familiar frame. Deviating too far from that frame may lead the text to be perceived as unsuccessful or even as a different genre entirely.

Viewing genres as frames (or even games) also allows us to take into account the knowledge that expert users bring to the production and reception of genres, and this knowledge is important because research suggests that both innovation and creativity require it. In other words, intentionally departing from norms requires an understanding of those norms. For example, writers must draw on their existing genre knowledge to determine what aspects of the genre they can bend or challenge and to gauge the degree to which they may depart from a prototype. Adapting a framework of multidimensional genre knowledge to the study of genre innovation may enable an analysis of the "innovation potential" of different aspects of genres in different sociocultural circumstances.

Social Environment

Whether we consider innovation in terms like alternatives, flouts, disruptions, or creativity, it is always dependent on markedness, unexpectedness, and unusualness. Therefore, we need to understand not only the "norms" and frames that are being bent or broken but also the community and context—the environment—in which such expectations were formed and have gained privileged status. Understanding environment, then, is essential in analyzing how judgments of innovation are reached (as opposed to judgments of deviation or transgressions), as innovation is better characterized as part of reader reception than as an inherent quality of a text. Furthermore, because perceptions of innovation are socially situated, they must also be considered dynamic (subject to change in different spatial and temporal contexts) and influenced by inequities and power structures. Judgments of innovation are further complicated in the case of texts that travel transnationally, or may have multiple (global) audiences and goals.

Readers' judgments of innovation may be additionally influenced by their perceptions of a text's author(s), including the author's experience and symbolic capital. Therefore, identity, voice, and ethos are all useful concepts for understanding how readers' may construct a writer and his or her legitimacy, authority, or right to innovate. Because a writer's roles, identities, and social power shift across environments and over time, these issues are again closely tied to social space.

An Example

To demonstrate how these principles can aid in understanding genre innovation, a quick example is useful, and for this I return to the lease-renewal letter discussed in Chapter 1 and shown in Figure 1.1. The author of this text clearly departs from expected convention, and yet the letter is effective. When I have shared the text with students or friends, they smile or even laugh out loud when they reach the final paragraph in the excerpt—this reaction is nearly unanimous. In other words, the text works, meeting our initial criterion for innovation: It is both novel and appropriate according to the intended readers.

What makes the text novel or original? First, it offers an element of surprise that unexpectedly embeds language more reminiscent of a friendly joke or email than that of a professional letter. The language includes hyperbole and repetition (". . . we truly, truly, truly hope . . ."), both of which are common strategies of language play. The content is also amusing, as a more conventional letter would simply perform a transactional function through impersonal language and would certainly not portray the company as having "feelings." The novelty, then, also stems from the mixing of discourses (professional and personal) within the genre's form and from the unexpected and uncommon content—and these two innovations work strategically together. Simply bringing in humorous content without the accompanying personal tone and hyperbole would be confusing rather than amusing to readers. Likewise, integrating personal language without the obviously unconventional content would seem odd as well.

We might characterize the innovations in this letter as flouts, or more specifically as "flagrant non-observances," following Greenall

(2009), as they are deliberate but are not explicitly called out to readers as violations. More broadly, we can apply a framework of discourse disruptions (Cook, 1994) to look at where the innovations occur in terms of level of schemata. In this case, we find disruptions primarily to language schemata. Alternatively, we can employ a genre knowledge framework to analyze the innovation, identifying such innovations as occurring within the genre's form, rhetorical strategies, and content. In the case of the lease-renewal letter, this latter framework seems to offers a bit more heuristic power.

Considering the social context in which the text was received allows for a richer analysis of the letter's innovations. First, it is noteworthy that the text does not bend the genre conventions until the readers have already established the purpose of the letter and confirmed its legitimacy as an example of the genre. In my own reception of the text, the letter was slipped under my apartment door in a business envelope that included the company's logo and address on the outside; the envelope also contained a lease renewal form (a legal document). The documents were delivered about two months prior to the end of my lease, so I was not surprised to receive them. Therefore, the letter was integrated within a recognizable network of genres and delivered in a recognizable manner, granting additional legitimacy to the text and framing my perceptions of what I was reading and how I should interpret it. Drawing on Bourdieu's (1991) model, then, the text satisfies for the typical reader the three "ritual conditions" needed to be recognized as authoritative: It is produced by a legitimate authority, within a legitimate situation, and in a legitimate form. Being granted authority, then, the text has earned social power and is perhaps freed up to depart from typical conventions. By the time the text does begin to bend the conventions of the genre, the reader has already established its legitimacy and identified its social action of requesting a lease renewal. The text follows enough of the genre's conventions that even the playful departures in the third paragraph do not alter the reader's interpretation of the text's purpose or social action, though they may change his or her reaction to the text. As predicted by creativity theory (Sawyer, 2012), the text does not depart so radically from the genre that it creates a new genre; instead, it departs enough to be a distinctive example of the same genre.

The innovations in the lease-renewal text may also be considered effective because they serve a particular rhetorical goal for the company. The intended readers (current tenants) would find the playful tone to be characteristic of the company's brand or identity. In providing tenants with unique perks like moving-in gifts or holiday doughnuts delivered to their doorways, the company in fact broke genre conventions in other situations as well. Departing from convention was part of the company's identity, serving as a kind of marketing strategy and branding itself as a playful, off-beat company—an image also communicated through the slogan of "city places for city people." Receiving the lease-renewal letter from this company would, then, be entirely different from receiving a letter like this from the Internal Revenue Service or from a lawyer. I immediately recognized the genre flouting as intentional and as part of the company's branded identity. As well, the lease-renewal letter is not a legal document in itself, and there are no external gatekeepers involved to sanction any departures from convention, so relatively fewer constraints are at play. The text might also be characterized as fairly low stakes—it is, after all, unlikely that a tenant would decide not to renew a lease based on the renewal letter alone, particularly as those receiving it will already be familiar with the company's brand identity.

This somewhat "quick and dirty" analysis illustrates just some of the ways in which the concepts outlined in this chapter and in Chapter 1 can help us analyze how innovation works within genres. The final section of this chapter outlines a more robust methodological approach to researching innovation.

Researching Innovation

Existing studies of innovation in writing have so far focused mostly on the text itself. While texts are indeed a crucial part of analysis, our theoretical exploration in this chapter demonstrates that such analysis should also consider elements like the possible intentions of the author, the text's purpose, and the social context and structures in which production, reception, and interpretation occur—all elements that cannot be found in text alone. The goal of this final section is to outline a range of methods and approaches that might be applied in the study of genre innovation. While the actual choice of approach will depend on the researcher's questions and goals, the descriptions given are intended to offer a guide for identifying possible methods that, when adopted in different studies over time, will help build our understanding of genre in more complex ways. I categorize these approaches into three general areas: text, social environment, and reception.

Text

Text analysis is often an important starting place for the study of genre innovation. Comparing traditional forms or common genre conventions to innovative texts can help reveal where the innovation occurs, how frequently, and how far from a prototype the text lies. Text analysis might include move analysis, in which researchers identify conventional moves and their sequences and then look for variations to these typicalities in innovative texts. With the lease-renewal letter, for example, move analysis would reveal the use of a completely unexpected move (Guilt the Tenant into Renewal?). Text-based studies of innovation have also, as we've already discussed, focused on the existence of language play in innovative texts, identifying the different strategies of play or inventiveness used. In her study of retention-promotion-tenure reports, for example, Hyon (2008) identified instances of inventive elements that "inject playfulness into these otherwise serious reports" (p. 182). After identifying these elements, she categorized them into three overlapping categories: hyperbole, irony-humor, and informal language. This approach of beginning with a type of rhetorical effect (e.g., inventiveness) and then identifying elements that contribute to it recalls literary or stylistic analysis, but, as Hyon demonstrates, can be quite useful even in academic genres.

Corpus-based text analysis also holds some promise for studying innovation or creativity in text. So far, Hyland's (2008, 2010) work, comparing lexico-grammatical features in a corpus of work by an individual author to a corpus of work from the author's disciplinary community, offers one of the few examples of this methodology. While Hyland uses corpus analysis to examine authorial identity, it has some potential for analyzing innovation; after all, in both cases, we are interested in understanding departures or deviations from a broader community norm. A key distinction, however, is that in Hyland's work the goal is to identify consistent and regular patterns *within* an author's writing and to compare those patterns to broader disciplinary conventions; but while an author's idiolect or stylistic "fingerprint" is detectable across many texts, innovation may be a one-time occurrence for an author, a rhetorical choice made to suit a very particular situation. So, while corpus analysis is extremely helpful in identifying conventional patterns of lexico-grammatical features, quantitative comparisons between text features in a single text and those in a large corpus of texts is somewhat problematic. That said, corpus descriptions of a genre may provide a useful starting place for understanding convention and therefore for identifying instances of obvious divergence. If a corpus analysis of biology articles, for example, finds an extremely low occurrence of quotations, we would have some indication that a biology article with several prominently placed quotations would be somewhat of an anomaly or a marked deviation.

Finally, textual analysis could focus on atypical use of rhetorical strategies within a genre. For example, the presence of personal stories, the use of statistics, or the use of emotional visuals are primarily rhetorical in nature and could all be areas of potential deviation. Canagarajah's (2006b) analysis of research article introductions across languages and audiences is one illustration of this kind of rhetorical analysis. Canagarajah demonstrates a Tamil scholar's adoption of a "civic ethos," "humility ethos," and/or "academic ethos" in texts written in Tamil, in English for a local audience, and in English for an international audience. Again, Canagarajah is not explicitly researching innovation here, but his analytic method could certainly be applied to analyzing genre innovation. Researchers might, for instance, identify conventional patterns of ethos or other rhetorical appeals, and then look for departures from those conventions in non-traditional texts. Canagarajah's analysis suggests that this could be a particularly fruitful approach to looking at unexpected departures that occur as a result of authors "shuttling between languages" and of readers orienting to particular linguistic and cultural expectations.

Social Environment

If our main goal is to understand the ways in which a text might depart from conventions of form, we might focus our analysis at the textual level. If, however, we want to know more about the functions of an innovative text (intended and unintended), the dynamics of production and reception of the innovative text, or the power structures that influence these other areas, we need to zoom out for a wider contextual view. Here, we might take a cue from language/discourse and creativity research, which offers some useful methodological arguments, if not specific examples. As mentioned earlier, both Carter (2007) and Jones (2010) strongly advocate for the use of ethnographic approaches in studying creativity, noting the value of such approaches for capturing and exploring the social environments and processes of innovation. For Jones, who sees creativity as "residing not in language but in the actions people take with language" (p. 472), ethnography can help re-focus analysts' attention to practices rather than strictly on text. Blommaert (2005) similarly sees ethnography, or "the ethnographic-sociolinguistic analysis of discourse" (p. 16), as a crucial approach to understanding the different interacting layers of discourse.

Given the situatedness of innovation, case studies—particularly longitudinal ones—also have strong potential as a methodology. Though there are few, if any, examples available for using case studies to understand innovation, scholarship in both academic writing and genre studies demonstrates their value more generally—Casanave's (2002) book *Writing Games* is an especially strong case in point. Such an approach could also be useful for understanding how reactions to innovative texts may change over time or for following individuals' approaches to innovation in target genres over time, giving insight into the relationship between genre knowledge and innovation.

Another macro-level approach to studying innovation can be found in creativity research and the sociocultural systems–based view (Csikszentmihalyi, 1999), briefly summarized earlier in this chapter. Though the systems approach is presented as a model rather than a methodology, its emphasis on social environment gives it strong potential for designing contextually oriented research and for organizing and interpreting data. In this model, creativity is defined as a process that emerges through the interaction of individuals, fields, and domains (see Figure 2.1).

Csikszentmihalyi (1999) outlines several questions that researchers might use to study the ways in which individuals, fields, and domains affect the creative process. For example, to understand how individuals' personal backgrounds affect their creativity, we might inquire about their family or community, their traditions for learning, the mentoring and support structures available to them, and the extent to which their background encouraged conformity or innovation. To learn about how the field and society influence creativity, we could consider where the society's energy is invested, the extent to which it values innovation, the allowance for change within the social economy, and the complexity of the social system (p. 322). In exploring the domain's role in creativity or innovation, we might examine its stage of development and history, accessibility, integration with other domains, or openness to other cultures (p. 318).

As may be obvious at this point, a disadvantage to the systems approach is its expansiveness. Where does one draw the observational and analytical boundaries of the relevant system? It is also a methodologically ambitious approach, possibly requiring historical,

Figure 2.1. A Systems Model of Creativity (Csikszentmihalyi, 1999, p. 315)

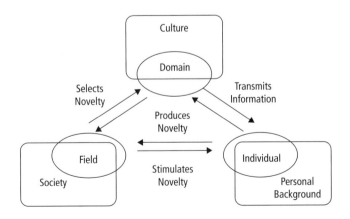

textual, and contextual ethnographic research all at once. Further, it may encourage relatively static or homogenous views of social groups such as "cultures" or "fields." Despite these limitations for researchers, the model has value in identifying some of the interacting features of innovation within a social context that might be as broadly construed as "an academic setting" or as specific as an undergraduate biology classroom or an international research group.

Reception

One subset of environmentally oriented approaches includes studies that focus specifically on the reception of texts. Reception is essential to the study of genre innovation because reader's responses give rise to judgments of innovation. An emphasis on reception has not been prominent in research of academic writing more generally, but Paul, Charney, and Kendall (2001) make a convincing case for its role, and Swales (2004) has echoed their sentiment. Focusing on rhetoric of science scholarship, the authors argue that the bulk of research in this area focuses on the historical circumstances leading up to the moment of reception—that is, the social and historical processes of production—but fails to examine a text's uptake in a meaningful way. Yet looking at how a text is received over time can lead to greater insight regarding the success or failure of its rhetorical strategies, or "the ultimate impact of a text on its readers" (Paul, Charney, & Kendall, 2001, p. 386). The authors outline several methods for reception studies, favoring approaches that blend textual analysis with reader focused meth ods, such as correlations between a text's subsequent citation rate and factors like author demographics or generic features of the text, peer review responses, think-aloud protocols with readers, or experimental studies of reader reactions to texts that conform to norms versus those that depart from norms.

Taking up the call for more reception-based studies of writing, Swales and Leeder (2012) analyzed characteristics of highly cited articles from the journal *English for Specific Purposes*. The authors combine analysis of citational uptake (i.e., later references to a published article) with genre analysis and interviews with the authors of highly cited articles. Challenging commonly held assumptions, Swales and Leeder found that the most highly cited articles in their corpus were authored by female, non-Anglophone scholars working in countries that do not dominate the publishing scene. Instead of demographic features playing a prominent role in uptake, the researchers identify three sociorhetorical factors that seem to be at play, including the authors' research approach, their objects of inquiry, and the perceived originality of their research at the time of publication. These successful articles, it seems "engender[ed] in their readers both a sense of recognition and a sense of surprise" (p. 145), suggesting that perceptions of newness, originality, and innovation were also at play.

Another approach to reception research can be found outside of writing or language studies in Michèle Lamont's (2009) investigations of academic judgment, summarized in her book *How Professors Think.* Lamont's interest is in understanding disciplinary preferences for judgments of quality, as well as where and how such evaluative norms are created. In studying the review process of national competitions for grants and fellowships in the humanities and social sciences in the United States, Lamont probes questions such as what "significance" or "originality" mean to reviewers in the context of academic evaluation. Her work bears relevance to genre innovation both methodologically and theoretically. For example, her method of observing review panels' deliberations and interviewing the peer reviewers, panelist chairs, and program officers shortly after such deliberations have taken place can be utilized in reception studies more broadly as a way to learn more about how individuals construct concepts like innovation and creativity, or deviation and transgression. This research approach further sheds lights on some of the important distinctions in disciplinary values regarding academic quality or the ways in which elements like cultural capital or social networks may influence judgments.

These three relatively recent works on reception offer useful examples for studying how judgments of innovations to genres are made. In addition, ethnographic analyses of both production and reception can further develop our contextual understanding of innovation. Combining a range of methods—including textual analysis, ethnography, and reception-based studies—allows for a robust means of studying some of the questions I take up in this book, such as who can innovate and when, or how possibilities for innovation may depend on characteristics of the genre and its social circumstances.

Taken together, the theoretical and methodological tools explored in this chapter provide a starting point for more in-depth studies of innovation within and through genres. I have not attempted to offer a single framework for such study but rather to present options that may be adapted to more specific investigations. Some of these tools, in other words, will be more appropriate for researching certain aspects of innovation over others. Studies of innovative forms, innovative processes, reception and effects of innovation, innovation and power, or innovation and knowledge do share some theoretical concepts but with distinct goals as well. While the various approaches explored in this chapter should by no means be considered comprehensive, they do demonstrate the ways in which research into genre innovation can draw on existing scholarship while extending that work in new and exciting ways. In the following chapters, I offer some examples of how these tools may be productively used. Chapter 3 explores genre innovation specifically within the context of academic writing and research, drawing on concepts such as flouting, language play, and social power to build a possible framework for understanding genre innovation within an ecosocial system—that framework is applied in Chapter 4 as a way to understand innovation and creativity in an undergraduate environmental science course. Chapter 5 picks up further on research of language play and alternative discourses and also adapts the analytic framework from Chapter 3 as a tool for raising students' genre awareness.

Chapter 3

Innovation in Academic Research Genres

So far, we have considered innovation and genre at a fairly general level, including public, personal, professional, and academic genres. This broad approach is a useful starting point, but because communities and spaces may differ in their reasons for, opportunities for, and constraints against innovation, a more community-specific analysis is also necessary. In this chapter, then, I shift to considering innovation in academic research genres. In doing so, I hope to highlight not only some of the reasons why academics—from students to top scholars—might choose to depart from generic norms but also some of the elements of the academic sociocultural system that influence the possibilities for and nature of innovation. Given the privileged status of academic genres in education and professional life, a more in-depth exploration of innovation in academe would seem to have important pedagogical implications. Though I take up a more detailed discussion of those implications in Chapter 5, this chapter lays the groundwork for the study of academic genre innovation.

Functions of Genre Innovation in Academic Research

Academic writing comes in a variety of genres, from student essay to refereed journal article to grant proposal. Though purposes and readers vary, many academic genres are evaluated by readers who determine whether a desired outcome has been achieved—a high grade, publication, or project funding, for example. Academic writers, then, typically have a vested interest in satisfying their readers, and this often means meeting readers' genre expectations. Given the potential risks of departing from convention in academic environments, a logical place to begin this chapter is by considering the question of *why* academic writers innovate. Why not simply write a traditional, "safe" text that adheres to readers' expectations?

There are plenty of reasons that academics and students might intentionally manipulate genres, perhaps most obviously to make their work stand out. All instances of genre, after all, display some variation, and often the most successful texts are those with noticeable departures from convention. But more specifically, what do writers aim to achieve through such departures? If genres are to be considered social actions, following Miller's (1984) now canonical phrase, they are produced in order to *do* something, to accomplish some sort of goal, to carry out a function or set of functions. Authors' decisions to violate or bend expected patterns must therefore be motivated by a purpose or set of purposes that extends beyond just appearing different. A comprehensive list of such purposes would be impossible to create, so I focus here instead on outlining some of the most common functions of innovation in academic genres.

Alternative Ways of Knowing

One common function of innovation in academic genres is primarily ideational: to facilitate the use of alternative or unconventional approaches to knowledge construction. Beliefs about what knowledge is and how it is constructed, or *epistemological styles* (a term adopted from Lamont, 2009), often become so embedded within a discipline that they are viewed not as preferences but simply as disciplinary practice, normalized ways of acting within the community. Disciplinary epistemological styles are a crucial component of the study of academic genres because the two are co-constitutive, shaping and structuring each other. The traditional scientific research article, for example, largely reflects the scientific method and its positivist paradigm that values objectivity, empirical observation, and deductive logic. It is challenging to stray radically from this approach to inquiry while writing within a traditional introduction-methods-research-discussion (IMRD) article format, which is at least in part why the IMRD structure is not adopted in humanities disciplines, where different epistemologies are valued.

While disciplinary epistemological styles serve important stabilizing purposes for a community, they simultaneously discourage divergent practices and alternative approaches to knowledge construction. As a result, adopting unconventional epistemologies becomes not just a socially risky endeavor but also a generically difficult one, as doing so requires challenging the associated genres. That said, researchers can and do explore new approaches to knowledge construction and by doing so engage in genre innovation. Despite the risks and challenges, alternative epistemological approaches offer the possibility of new insights into disciplinary problems and therefore carry the potential for making significant contributions to a field. Such approaches may include methods of inquiry that a researcher adopts and/or the forms for presenting and sharing that research with the larger community.

The adoption of an unconventional research approach can be an especially bold move, as methodology is deeply engrained in academic community culture. While some uncommon research approaches or methods may still align well within prevailing knowledge paradigms, others may be more radical, challenging basic disciplinary beliefs about how new knowledge is (or should be) acquired. Sociologists Miller and Tewksbury (2001) characterize such radical methodological departures in their area of crime and deviance as "extreme methods"—highly unusual or creative approaches to inquiry, such as covert participant observation in environments like prisons or inner-city gangs. As these researchers note, extreme research methods are professionally precarious because they challenge disciplinary dogmas and may therefore be shunned by peers and funding agencies. But methods that are not shut out (perhaps are not so extreme as to raise the hackles of the gatekeepers) may be heralded as novel and thus rewarded for their contributions. And such innovations may also serve, eventually, to challenge or even change generic practices. An anthropologist in Thaiss and Zawacki's (2006) study, for example, reflects on his post-modern ethnography of the Sandinista revolution, which he considered extremely risky and "against the grain" (p. 44) at the time it was published but that is now mainstream in anthropology. Adopting less traditional approaches to research may carry special risks for graduate students, who have yet to establish themselves in their field and are still subject to the pressures of defending a dissertation, publishing for the first time, and securing a job. Despite these pressures, though, some doctoral students do turn to alternative approaches of inquiry because they see such approaches as the most appropriate ones for their research questions (Belcher & Hirvela, 2005; Casanave, 2010).

One example of innovative methodology in the sciences is *citizen science*—an approach to scientific research that directly involves the public in gathering, discussing, and sometimes even analyzing data. One of the first examples of citizen science is the SETI(Search for Extraterrestrial Intelligence)@home project, based at the University of California–Berkeley. When the researchers faced the problem of accessing enough computing power for their large-scale analyses, they sought a solution in the thousands of small home computers throughout the United States. As described on their website, the project "hopes to convince you to allow us to borrow your computer when you aren't using it and to help us '. . . search out new life and new civilizations'" (Hipschman, n.d.). The project has been successful in convincing *netizens* to get involved: since 1999, more than six million volunteers have participated (Korpela et al., 2011).

While SETI@home looks to the general public for the use of computer power, citizen science projects have also enlisted public volunteers as data collectors and processors. In France, the French Breeding Bird Survey (FBBS) uses amateur birdwatchers to monitor a plot for several years following a standardized protocol; 1,300 volunteers have participated in the project since 2001 (Jiguet et al., 2012). The Whale FM project looks to the general public for help with analyzing its database of nearly 15,000 audio recordings of whale calls—a data set far too vast for a small team of researchers to tackle. Citizen scientists can visit the project's website, hosted by the journal *Scientific American*, listen to a small subset of calls, and indicate any close matches that they perceive; in essence, these public research assistants are helping to classify the recordings, "casting a vote for those two calls to be considered 'similar'" (Zooniverse, 2011). While these innovative research approaches help scientists cope with developing and analyzing extremely large sets of data, they do not conform to many of the traditional doctrines of experimental research and thus challenge conventional and familiar epistemologies. As a report on the FBBS project demonstrates, research articles arising out of citizen science are also likely to depart somewhat from tradition, with extra attention being paid to the method and often advocating for continued use of such studies. Unusually, the FBBS article also includes an acknowledgement in which the paper "is dedicated to all volunteers who participate to the national breeding bird survey" (Jiguet et al., 2012, p. 65).

Alternative methods of inquiry may lead to generic forms that are perceived as innovative, but the reverse may also occur, as in the case of researchers who begin with innovative forms for sharing their work and, as a result, are able to draw on new ways of knowing. Because of the mutually constitutive relationship between genre form and knowledge construction, the adoption of an unconventional text may open up novel ways of thinking about one's research. Bizzell (2002) argues that innovative forms of discourse "allow their practitioners to do intellectual work in ways they could not if confined to traditional academic discourse" (p. 3). As one small example, the simple incorporation of the first-person pronoun *I* may allow authors to emphasize their own role in knowledge construction, from research design through interpretation, an ideological move that may be curtailed by adhering to more traditional conventions that discourage self-referential pronouns. In their study of postmodern humanities theses, Starfield and Ravelli (2006) found that a reflexive use of *I* may be used by writers to articulate their own social and political situatedness within the research and the research process, as in this example:

> The writing of this thesis was a process that *I could not explore* with the positivistic detachment of the classical sociologist. After all, *I was affected* by the repression, the exile and the mutations within Chilean society as much as anyone else in the country. (p. 234, emphasis in original)

One example of innovation at the discourse level of the presentation of academic research is the strategy of hybridizing or mixing genres in perhaps unexpected ways. In their co-authored chapter, for example, Paul Kei Matsuda and Dwight Atkinson (2008) eschew a conventional approach to form and announce this intent explicitly to their readers, as in Greenall's (2009) strategy of "opting out," described in Chapter 2. They explain: "Because contrastive rhetoric (CR) may be at a crucial point in its history—one which requires substantial rethinking of nearly everything associated with it—we decided to match this exploratory moment with an equally exploratory genre: the academic conversation" (p. 277). Their chapter is fronted with a brief introduction that situates their conversation as having taken place "on the evening of September 25, 2004, before a warm fire in an old house on Deer Isle, Maine, USA" (p. 277) and then continues as a discussion between the two authors as they reflect on CR as an area of inquiry. Aside from being presented structurally as a dialogue in which the authors probe and play off of each other's thoughts, the text is marked by personal stories and reflections, interrogatives, a few conversational interruptions, and even references to the composing process (e.g., "But I'm falling asleep so let's start to wrap this up. This is my last beer." p. 297)—all features that are rare in traditional academic book chapters. Yet, the text still adopts many features that are characteristic of academic discourse, such as lengthy sentences, jargon, citations, the use of complete sentences, and a general lack of slang or colloquialisms. By mixing genres (interview/dialogue and scholarly article), the authors attempt to construct knowledge dialogically as they offer new insights into where the field of CR has been and where it might be headed.

The academic memoir or autobiography is another example of generic hybridization that offers opportunities for new ways of knowing—examples that readers might be familiar with include Clifford Geertz's (2000) *Available Light,* Johns Swales' (2009) *Incidents in an Educational Life,* Stephanie Vandrick's (2009) *Interrogating Privilege,* and Victor Villanueva's (1993) *Bootstraps.* Blending autobiographical reflection with disciplinary exploration while establishing the author's place as a senior member of a field, such memoirs carry out multiple social actions that would not be possible through a research article, a traditional scholarly book, or even a traditional autobiography; the mixing of genres allows for new insights into disciplinary issues, and it does so through stories that are engaging, compelling, and memorable (Nash,

2004; Vandrick & Casanave, 2014). In a refereed journal article that blends the academic autobiography with case study research, Gentil and Serór (2014) show the potential of such layered hybridization for reaching new knowledge. Sharing their own personal autobiographies and paths to biliteracy, Gentil and Serór analyze their histories within existing scholarly conversations on writing for publication. Their work is a blend of convention and innovation that mixes traditional use of discourse structures, visual displays of data, terminology, and analysis with personal stories, the use of first names, and less conventional methodology. Injecting the personal into the academic and exploiting their own first-hand knowledge as biliterate applied linguists, the authors are able to provide insights that would be impossible through more traditional case study research. Their work reflects Pennycook's (2012) assertion that "to write in unexpected ways is to engage in a reflexive struggle over text" (p. 35). In the case of the academic autobiography or memoir, a new genre seems to have been established, so that we have a name for it and even some recognizable patterns, though it is still characterized by a high degree of variation.

Hybridization is just one example of the use of alternative generic forms as a means of adopting new approaches to knowledge construction. Aware that conventional genres shape thinking in particular ways, authors may choose to create altogether new forms or to appropriate existing non-academic genres into academic settings. For example, Vershawn Young, a U.S. compositionist, has utilized performance art as a means of exploring language, rhetoric, and racial identities for academic and public audiences. Similarly, a 2011 conference for the American Comparative Literature Association, ACL(x), asked participants to share their work in any form *other than* the traditional 20-minute read-aloud paper, with the goal of "explor[ing] new possibilities for the production and distribution of scholarly knowledge in the conference setting—'new' in (for instance) format, technological basis, mode of participation, or output" (ACLA, n.d.). These kinds of experimentations with generic norms are motivated by a desire to try out new options for knowledge construction by leaving the perceived straitjacket of genre behind and, potentially, offering significant contributions to scholarship.

Self-Expression and Reader Engagement

A second common function of innovation in academic genres is more interpersonal in nature: to present oneself in particular ways and/or to engage readers. While these goals may be distinct for some writers, they work to both personalize and build reader-writer interaction within genres that are typically (or stereotypically) thought of as impersonal and distant. This impression of academic writing as a relatively sterile discourse is in many ways rooted in conventions like a heavy use of jargon, the need to situate one's work within a larger citational network, and a general avoidance of informal (and, therefore, conversation-like) elements of communication. To flout such conventions allows writers to express themselves in unexpected, perhaps even unique, ways while drawing readers in to the text through the disruptions to traditional discourse patterns.

When academic writers adhere rigidly to genre conventions, they create (intentionally or not) a certain impression of themselves as writers. They may project, for example, an image of a traditional, knowledgeable, and fairly experienced member of a discipline, someone who is familiar with the social system and expectations. But sometimes a writer may not want to emphasize conformity, choosing instead to highlight his or her individuality even as it is projected within a social system. One strategy for such self-expression is to bend or flout convention; in doing so, the text becomes marked in certain ways, drawing the reader's attention to the text and its author (Matsuda & Tardy, 2007)—to return to Cook's discussion of discourse disruption (see Chapter 2), we might understand this as "schema refreshing discourse." Some minor departures from convention may be expected (even, paradoxically, conventional) within academic genres; a personal website, for example, relies on the presence of at least some expression of individuality in order to be effective. But other academic genres are less overt about identity projection, and it is in these kinds of texts that self-expression through genre bending may be a more innovative and risky endeavor.

In previous research, for instance, I followed a graduate student writer ("John") who repeatedly bent or stretched conventions as a means of taking ownership over genres and representing himself as an individual—albeit one working within a disciplinary system (Tardy, 2005). One such example was found in a set of presentation slides he created for a biomedical engineering course project on cochlear implants. In contrast to the bright-colored background with geometrical shapes traditionally used in science and engineering slides, John created a template with a white background and a faded watermark image of the inner ear, a visual design that he considered to be atypical in his discipline. He explained:

> Well, for my personal style, I usually avoid really hard styles. Like, in engineering, they typically have a blue background with, like, "Purdue University" and have a Purdue mark and something underneath, and go with that. And that's what you see for most every—that's *really* conservative. And most PowerPoint slides are based on that and just diverge a little, but I usually change it a lot to get more visual attention from the people who are looking at the presentation. (Tardy, 2005, pp. 332–333)

John's shift in visual style was subtle but purposeful and served, as he states, to portray him as less conservative and to grab the attention of his audience.

This example illustrates how student writers may strive to play with generic expectations for the purposes of self-expression, and we can certainly find even more such instances among academic writers who have reached the tops of their field. Given their accumulated symbolic capital, these expert writers may be even freer to manipulate generic expectations, drawing on or recombining symbolic resources in less traditional ways through their stylistic, methodological, and even topical choices. By challenging conventions, writers find ways not only to perform identities and individual styles but also to build *ethos*. As they demonstrate knowledge of how to depart from convention effectively, writers can establish themselves as having experience and credibility—a strategy that, as we explored in Chapter 2, may in turn influence readers' judgments of a text as innovative rather than deviant.

As with John's presentation slide design, such stylistic departures not only allow the writer to express him- or herself in ways perceived as new or different but also, through these unexpected innovations, draw readers in. In the university retention-promotion-tenure (RPT) evaluations that Hyon (2008) studied, inventive language carried out these same functions of self-expression and reader engagement, as in these RPT text excerpts:

> Student response to Professor X's teaching is astonishingly positive. In the winter of 1997 X's English 311 class gave X rather average (for the "school") SETEs—not bad, for a large required class that students *dread*, but human. Since then X's SETE results *have levitated into a kind of superhuman empyrean*. Several classes . . . rate the "overall quality of instruction" 4.00. (Department Committee) (Hyon, 2008, p. 183, emphasis in original)

> X's recent participation in a three-week French immersion class in Quebec has done more than lead to *X babbling French in the corridors of University Hall*; X kept a journal of X's experiences and plans to incorporate . . . insights into X's undergraduate and graduate classes in language acquisition—further evidence of X's ability to link experience and pedagogy. (Department Committee) (Hyon, 2008, p. 184, emphasis in original)

While these italicized expressions certainly lend the text a unique identity, portraying the authors (English professors) as witty and verbally endowed academics, Hyon points out that they also entertain readers and bring some fun to the otherwise serious task of peer evaluation. In doing so they may too build solidarity with readers—including the faculty member being evaluated—within the potentially face-threatening act of performance review.

The issue of reader engagement (or lack thereof) has been of particular interest to many scholars who have criticized academic writing as typically bland, unnecessarily wordy, and often impenetrable (e.g., Limerick, 1993; Sword, 2009). The decision to write in a more "reader-friendly" manner is often characterized by these critics as innovative precisely *because* it departs from the more common conventions. Christine Pearson Casanave, a longtime advocate for a more accessible and engaging approach to academic writing, puts the argument this way: "Scholarly work that makes us want to turn pages *is* important. It is a futile exercise to work for years on a project that will not be read, or if read, will not be read with interest and engagement by evaluators and other readers" (Casanave, 2010, p. 12).

Helen Sword (2009), an educational scholar, has similarly lamented the conventional language of academic journal articles. Her graduate students, she argues, "want stories, examples, ideas, solutions—not long parenthetical references, convoluted flowcharts and truckloads of educational jargon" (p. 319). In her quest to locate accessible and engaging educational research articles, Sword compared the texts of 100 journal articles in higher education with the texts of 10 writers identified by her colleagues as "the most stylish writers" in the field. Perhaps the most interesting aspect of Sword's study is not the results (on her 10-point scale, the "stylish" writers fell in a respectable range of 8 to 10 while the journal articles averaged just 1.32) but her approach to sharing those results. Sword presents her research and its findings in two separate versions within the same journal article. The first version adopts a traditional IMRD structure, packed with lengthy sentences, extensive citations, graphs, and passive voice; the study's results are discussed in relation to each research question. The second, more innovative, version does not include a separate introduction or methods section, instead jumping right into the findings, which are ordered this time by topic, comparing the journal articles and stylish writers in terms of several aspects of the prose, such as titles, stories, jargon, interdisciplinarity, and creativity and engagement. In addition to its innovative structure (which would doubtless face challenges getting through the editorial gate of many journals), Sword's second version is marked by frequent use of *I* ("With pleasure and pride, I realised that I had finally passed through the Pearly Gates of professional competence" [p. 329]), rhetorical questions ("What are these two articles really about?" [p. 325]), personal stories and anecdotes, and extended metaphors. In her conclusion, Sword does acknowledge the riskiness of her second approach and of unconventional academic writing more generally, noting that readers' responses to her pre-published article were mixed at best. Yet, she argues, such mixed reception demonstrates that the point is not the nature of readers' reactions but simply that they *have* strong reactions, that they are engaged in the text.

So far, we've considered how innovations to genre might be used for interpersonal functions like writer self-expression or reader engagement. A related purpose here combines attention to the writer and to the reader—that is, innovations may serve to build rapport between the two. As previously mentioned, Hyon (2008) has argued that playful innovations in evaluative genres may also function to express solidarity with the person being evaluated, and Swales (2004) notes a similar function for the use of humor in dissertation defenses. In both of these cases, humor or playfulness (unconventional to academic genres) may reduce tension for participants who are placed in hierarchical and evaluative roles. Some explanation for the use of this kind of creative language is found in Carter's (2004) corpus-based study of everyday talk. Carter found creativity (defined primarily as language play) to be more prevalent in personal conversations among friends and family than in transactional conversations among non-intimate individuals. Perhaps it is in these more personal situations that we feel most comfortable putting convention aside, but doing so also seems to assist in building our relationships and collaborations.

Resistance and Change of Dominant Discourses

The interpersonal functions of innovation described may be important for writers who simply want to change their own writing and the ways in which readers engage with their texts. But the goals of innovation are at times more ambitious: to resist or even change the conventions of dominant discourses. Scholars who have advocated for more personal, accessible, and engaging academic prose often also express concern for the limitations and constraints of dominant discourses and hope that individual acts of resistance may eventually lead to an alteration of convention. After all, genres do change over time, prompted by shifts in communities, material realities, and social structures, but also by the individual willingness of some writers to depart from expected norms.

Genre innovation as an act of resistance reflects an intentional choice to reject dominant discourses, not simply because they may constrain knowledge production in some way but more specifically to subvert the structures of power that dominant discourses represent. In the world of academic research genres, for example, privileged norms are reinforced through guidebooks, style manuals, journal and book guidelines, graduate courses, and, of course, gatekeepers. Because such norms reflect particular worldviews, writers who are located at the community's margins may feel resistant to adopting such patterns. Students or disciplinary newcomers, for example, often feel alienated by the conventions of academic writing, which may seem disconnected from their own life experiences. In their well-known study of a new doctoral student, Berkenkotter, Huckin, and Ackerman (1988) show how "Nate" initially resisted the norms and conventions of his new disciplinary field of rhetoric and composition in favor of those from his prior disciplinary affiliations with education and with more expressivist orientations to rhetoric and composition. His early writing in his PhD program was therefore marked by "excessive" use of first person and "active, colorful verbs and metaphoric constructions" (p. 16). When reflecting on the process of assimilating his writing and thought to a new scientific epistemology, he likened the change to "a Frankensteinian notion of what will happen to my mind" (p. 18). Like many novices, Nate eventually did modify his writing to be more reflective of disciplinary norms, but not all newcomers choose this path.

Resistance to traditional genre expectations may also be attractive to scholars from marginalized ethnolinguistic communities who want to avoid being hemmed in by conventions created and maintained by dominant groups. Canagarajah (2002) has argued that "Periphery scholars" should "adopt a paradoxical attitude of resisting convention even as we communicate with them" (p. 85), creatively manipulating them to serve personal needs and objectives. He demonstrates this resistance through the example of a Tamil political scientist, Manivasakar, who adopts a high-involvement style in his academic writing, filled with hyperbole, rhyming, alliteration, puns, and parallelism, creating a polemical and oratorical style atypical of traditional academic prose:

> Speaking with ontological, epistemological and teleological implications, intellectual colonialism is not a mere manifestation of colonialism; is it the subtle, sinister and sophisticated instrument of (neo)colonialism to control and dominate the non-western world politically, economically, socially, culturally and psychologically by producing and exporting pseudo developmentalism. (Canagarajah, 2002, p. 150)

The text exemplifies what Canagarajah calls a "creative oppositional discourse," which negotiates dominant discourses with local discourses in effective ways. The key, Canagarajah (2002) argues, is not alienating the ("dominant Center") audience but taking their perspectives and expectations into consideration. Negotiation is thus an act of appropriation, making conventional discourses work for new purposes and infusing them with new ideologies.

Phan Le Ha (2009) writes of this same act of negotiation in reflecting on her role as a teacher and advisor. She describes herself as a "rebellious" writer but states that rather than simply rejecting dominant norms and expectations, she "acknowledge[s] and incorporate[s] them in both content and the form of my writing . . . not by imposing; rather, negotiation, mutual learning and community-building" (p. 137). Drawing on Kramsch (2001) and Bourdieu (1991), Phan Le Ha adopts a Thirdspace pedagogy that aims to help students not only learn the norms of power but also how to "gain a profit of distinction by using English in ways that are unique to their multilingual and multicultural sensibilities" (Kramsch, 2001, p. 16, cited in Phan Le Ha, 2009, p. 138). She describes assisting her student, Arianto, in gradually finding an effective balance between personal identity expression and scholarly engagement with existing literature through a process of moving from being colonized to self-colonization, to de-colonization and self-obsession, and finally to appropriation.

In some cases, resistance to existing norms may be motivated not just by self-expression of identity but also by a desire to change dominant conventions, or at least to open them up for a wider range of participants. Belcher (2009), for example, writes of the movement among feminist scholars to offer alternatives to the traditional agonistic, male-style discourse found in much academic writing. As Belcher notes, some marginalized scholars—whether marginalized by gender, ideology, or ethnolinguistic background—may accommodate different norms in different locales or may attempt to "nudge Anglophone discourse itself toward change by interpolating new hybrid styles into mainstream Anglophone academia" (p. 224). Geneva Smitherman is well known for her norm-resistant texts, which hybridize discourses and genres. Her 1976 article in *English Journal*, for example, blends African American Vernacular English with Standard English, colloquial language with academic discourse:

> In the English/language arts area, the challenge comes down to accepting the students' native language/dialect while simultaneously heightening their consciousness of the communications process and enhancing their capabilities therein. To cope with this brave new world of ours, students need knowledge of and performance competence in the use of language and meta-language as fundamental dynamics in social interaction. Now, didn't nobody say this was gon be easy to teach, but methinks English teachers is baaaaad enough to do it! And if some of y'all need some mo edumacation in this area, just pressure yo school system to provide a staff development program. (After all, they did it for the "new math.") (Smitherman, 1976, p. 14)

For Smitherman, such resistance is not merely decorative but effectively carries out her very argument that dominant norms need to be critically examined by students and teachers.

Common wisdom tells us that established scholars will often be granted the right to resist and innovate in the way that Smitherman does, but what about student writers or disciplinary newcomers, who lack the accumulated capital to break with expectations? While some successful examples of student resistance do exist in the literature (e.g., Canagarajah, 2013; Lu, 1994), they tend to take place within classrooms that are very open to—and perhaps encourage—such critical acts. Outside of such environments, reception of resistance by newcomers may be less positive, but it is certainly an area worthy of more research.

Critique

An extreme form of resistance includes overt critique of dominant discourses, practices, values, or epistemological styles. Unlike typical resistant acts, critique is more explicit and usually unambiguous. This use of genre flouting as a way to "fight the man" is what Dietel-McLaughlin (2009) labels "irreverent composition":

> Irreverent compositions may employ acts of imitation, such as parody or satire; additionally, these compositions may modify or stray from the standard conventions of a genre (be it a literary genre or the "genre" of an event or arena) in service of a rhetorical purpose. These strategies work as rhetorical tropes—commonly understood as being artful deviations from the norm—by disrupting audience expectations and institutionalized conventions in order to make a larger political statement. (p. 3)

As Dietel-McLaughlin notes, parody is a common example of critique, typically bringing to mind satirical news shows, movies, or comedy skits that are often political in nature. But interesting examples of parody can also be found in the academic world, such as the case of Harold Miner's (1956) article "Body Ritual among the Nacirema," originally published in *American Anthropologist*. The conventional nature of Miner's apparent ethnography is easily identified in these excerpts, which are representative of the entire text:

> Professor Linton first brought the ritual of the Nacirema to the attention of anthropologists twenty years ago (1936: 326), but the culture of this people is still very poorly understood. They are a North American group living in the territory between the Canadian Cree, the Yaqui and Tarahumare of Mexico, and the Carib and Arawak of the Antilles. (p. 503)

Nacirema culture is characterized by a highly developed market economy which has evolved in a rich natural habitat. (p. 503)

Every household has one or more shrines devoted to [cleansing rituals] . . . . While each family has at least one such shrine, the rituals associated with it are not family ceremonies but are private and secret . . . . I was able, however, to establish sufficient rapport with the natives to examine these shrines and to have the rituals described to me. (pp. 503–504)

Miner's use of common moves like indicating a research gap or describing his researcher status and his choice of typical anthropological expressions such as *shrine, rituals,* or *the natives* are conventional to the genre of ethnography at this time period. But, of course, Miner is not writing of an exotic tribe at all: His article describes Americans (the reverse spelling of Nacirema) and their odd obsession with personal hygiene. By turning a (very) familiar cultural group into the object of anthropological inquiry, Miner effectively demonstrates how such discourse defamiliarizes, exoticizes, and "others" the groups studied by anthropologists, thereby normalizing a particular ideology within the disciplinary field. In adopting a common genre frame but introducing unexpected content (and illustrating Pennycook's [2007] argument that sameness can create difference), Miner creates a subversive text that looks very traditional on the surface; in fact, the only obvious departure from convention here is his object of inquiry—a "developed" culture that is familiar to readers. With this small departure, Miner produces a highly innovative critique.

One of the best known academic examples of genre innovation for the purpose of critique is what has become known as "The Sokal Hoax." In the mid-1990s, an article by Alan Sokal, a New York University physicist, appeared in a special issue of the cultural studies journal *Social Text* (a non–peer reviewed journal at the time) on the theme "Science Wars." Sokal's (1996b) article, "Transgressing the Boundaries: Towards a Transformative Hermeneutics of Quantum Gravity," claims to bring together quantum theory and postmodern theory, appealing to an intellectual zeitgeist at that time. Shortly after the article was published, Sokal (1996a) outed it in a short piece appearing in *Lingua Franca,* calling the article a nonsensical parody, intentionally written to test "the prevailing intellectual standards" (Sokal, 2000, p. 49) of certain areas of the humanities—particularly American scholarship on postmodern theory. In his *Lingua Franca* article, Sokal asks:

> Would a leading North American journal of cultural studies—whose editorial collective includes such luminaries as Frederic Jameson and Andrew Ross—publish an article liberally salted with nonsense if (a) it sounded good and (b) it flattered the editors' ideological preconceptions? The answer, unfortunately, is yes. (2000, p. 49)

The rhetorical uptake of the text offers an instructive story of genre innovation. On the one hand, Sokal's article was published, implying either that the *Social Text* editors found it to be of publishable quality or that they were willing to overlook their inability to assess its quality because of their eagerness to publish a paper on this topic (Sokal contends it was the latter). It is possible that Sokal's adoption of disciplinary and genre conventions blinded the editors (and perhaps subsequent readers) to the meaningless content and true intent of the text. Sentences like those excerpted in Figure 3.1 (accompanied by Sokal's amusing [2008] commentary) give a flavor of the overall article—a relentless use of buzzwords, references to European (especially French) cultural theorists, and dense footnotes.

While Sokal questions how his paper could possibly have passed as well intentioned, its seemingly naive reception is not as straightforward as we might initially presume. As Kill (2008) demonstrates, the rhetorical context of the editors' reading of the text is an important factor. Sokal's submission would have come to the attention of the editors through a familiar chain of genres, including a submission letter that would give no indication of the manuscript's underlying intent. Furthermore, the editors would likely have welcomed a submission to their journal from a New York University science professor—particularly for a special issue on science—and would therefore be less likely to question the content of the paper. But in different rhetorical

Figure 3.1. Excerpts from Sokal's Original "Hoax" Text (and Footnotes) with His (2008) Commentary

Original Text	Sokal's (2008, p. 34) Commentary
As Althusser rightly commented, "Lacan finally gives Freud's thinking the scientific concepts that it requires".[59] More recently, *Lacan's topologie du sujet*	*In an early draft, I wrote "Lacan's topologico-psychosocial theory"; but one of my friends, Montse Domínguez, raised the very sensible questions: "What is that? And what does mathematical typology have to do with psychoanalysis, anyway?" And I began to worry that this passage might betray the hoax. But then I hit upon the perfect solution: to obfuscate the question and divert the reader from thinking, use French! (Well, use any foreign language—but Lacan is French.)*
has been applied fruitfully to cinema criticism[60] and to the psychoanalsysis of AIDS.[61]	*The reader may be wondering what, precisely, mathematical topology has to do with film criticism and "the psychoanalysis of AIDS". Well, so am I, even after reading the cited articles.*
In mathematical terms, Lacan is here pointing out that the first homology group[62] of the sphere is trivial, while those of the other surfaces are profound; and this homology is linked with the connectedness or disconnectedness of the surface after one or more cuts.	*This last word is a joke: "trivial" is here a technical term in mathematics (meaning "the group consisting only of the identity element"); its correct antonym is "nontrivial", not "profound".*

contexts, Kill argues, the text's meanings become ambiguous, taken up in distinct ways. For those reading an apparently conventional text (at least in form), received and disseminated through conventional processes, the parody is not visible. The innovation for these readers was located instead in the text's unique exploration of postmodernism by a practicing scientist. But for those in on the hoax—including Sokal but also those of us who know of the paper only because of its eventual exposure—the innovation lies elsewhere, in its surreptitious adoption of convention through blatantly absurd content.

Though it is arguably a unique and rare case, the Sokal Hoax does demonstrate the crucial importance of reception in genre innovation. Bhatia (1993, 2004) has long argued that genres carry out a range of both public and more hidden, private intentions, and Sokal's paper shows us that the interpretation of such intentions is rarely clear-cut. When critiquing institutions through generic departures (whether stylistic, conceptual, or procedural), writers may not always want their true intention to be visible—at least not by those in power. While the parodic critiques described in this section are extreme examples aimed at relatively large audiences, most readers have probably anecdotally heard of colleagues writing near-parodies for various professional purposes or of students doing the same to satisfy paper requirements that they feel are unreasonable and/or not worthy of their true investment. Indeed, some readers may themselves have adopted a parodic approach to their own academic writing in some circumstances as a more subtle or private form of critique.

A Multiplicity of Functions

The previous sections have categorized functions of genre innovation as a means for exploring the actions and motives that such convention-departures may seek to carry out. As is generally the case, these categories are not intended to be distinct. Texts can and do carry out multiple functions and intentions, and certainly innovations in a text may aim to explore new approaches to knowledge construction, engage readers, *and* resist or critique dominant discourses. Malcolm Ashmore's (1989) *The Reflexive Thesis,* for example, seems to perform many if not all of these functions. Ashmore's text, published by University of Chicago Press in its original dissertation form, subverts numerous dissertation conventions; while writing on the very topic of self-reflection in the sociology of scientific knowledge, Ashmore, in effect, turns his argument to the dissertation genre itself, finding a novel way to explore and present his academic argument. But this approach may also reflect some proclivities of the author, as Ashmore employs a similar strategy in the abstract of a co-authored introduction article in a journal special issue:

> In this introduction, we attempt to convey something of the *angst* we have experienced at various times during the long drawn out process of being commissioned as Editors of this Special Issue, of commissioning authors and thereafter variously exhorting, encouraging and congratulating them (at a crucial stage, when the whole thing had got too big and the consulting referees had reported, being obliged to reject the efforts of some potential contributors); engaging the services of said referees, and later, with some difficulty, negotiating with them the continuation of the project; and finally, after an incredibly intense period of solid wall-to-wall subediting on the final drafts (Ashmore) and the writing of this introduction (Richards), finding it all, almost, over; at last, at last! This is attempted through the deployment of an extended narrative metaphor which likens our field to a restaurant, and a lyrical code celebrating anticlimax.
>
> We also manage to introduce the papers. (Richards & Ashmore, 1996, p. 219)

Are we to read the abstract as a humorous parody? An edgy critique? An attempt to engage and entertain readers? We can certainly imagine the authors entertaining themselves while writing it, and that in itself brings a certain life to the text. The excerpt stands as a good example of how the functions of innovations within and through genre are probably rarely straightforward but instead multiple and even open to divergent interpretations by readers in different environments, with distinct intentions and backgrounds themselves.

The Role of Intention in Innovation

These discussions of the various functions that innovation can serve in academic genres have largely presumed some degree of authorial intention. Whether relative novices or experts, the authors in these examples aim to carry out certain motives by departing from expected frames and conventions. At the same time, as described in Chapter 1, the definition of genre innovation that I have drawn upon does not assume authorial intention, but rather places emphasis on the reception of a text. In some cases, there may be tension between a text's reception and the author's intended effect, and this tension is itself useful for understanding genre innovation. Authors may intend to largely conform to convention but instead fail to satisfy the expectations of their audience. Such generic performances may be disregarded as weak or uninformed and might mark the author as an outsider or novice.

Other instances of genre might be considered innovative by readers but were produced with a more conventional intent. In presenting workshops on teaching second language writing, for example, I often share sample literacy narratives by multilingual writers as an object of discussion with teachers or tutors. I have been struck by how frequently workshop participants praise the "spice," "flavor," or "voice" of these student papers. When I ask them to point to something that led them to characterize the writing in this way, they typically refer to unique idiomatic expressions or word choices that have been translated directly from the author's native language, or to one writer's use of Chinese proverbs or fables. These instances of language and genre become, for some readers, examples of creativity, marked by unexpected or non-traditional forms. What is less clear, though, is whether the authors intended for their texts to be marked or creative in this way; in some cases, having worked closely with the student writers, I believe that this was not the intent.

This example demonstrates the interesting dialogic and situated nature of innovation. Blommaert (2010) argues that such tension in perceptions of creativity is to some degree expected in today's highly mobile and globalized world. As he writes:

> As we now know, globalization creates a heightened salience for the nature and structure of linguistic resources. As soon as linguistic semiotic products start travelling across the globe, they travel across different orders of indexicality, and what counts as "good language" in one place can easily become "bad language"

in another; what counts as an expression of deference can become an expression of arrogance elsewhere; what counts as an index of intellectual middle-class identity in one place can become an index of immigrant underclass identity elsewhere. (p. 127)

The social identities of language users may come to bear on such judgments as well. In my own research into reader constructions of authorial voice, I found that such indexing was often unpredictable among readers (Tardy, 2012b). For example, one multilingual student's academic paper used informal phrases like "a guy named Wichert" (referring to another author) and "tons of websites." For some readers, these phrases indicated an unsophisticated or novice writer, while for others the word choices suggested a writer who was willing to take risks in trying to manipulate academic conventions for personal intent. These mixed reactions are explained by Blommaert (2010) as a feature of mobility. As people move across spaces and "orders of indexicality" (see Chapter 2), communication (including reception of genres) becomes "much less predictable than what would happen in 'their own' environment" (Blommaert, 2010, p. 41). It is for this reason that he argues for a sociolinguistics that takes a systems perspective to understand the interrelations and connections among social systems of language users. In the same spirit, I now turn to such a perspective for understanding genre innovation.

Understanding Academic Genre Innovation Ecologically

As the previous sections suggest, to gain an adequate understanding of genre innovation, including the possibilities and constraints at play, we need to understand the wider social environment in which the innovation occurs. The systems-based approach described in Chapter 2 offers one tool for understanding that environment and the interactions of individuals within it. The principle behind systems-based thinking is that because a system is made up of complex, interacting elements, as relationships and purposes change, the system itself changes (Meadows, 2008); in other words, to understand changes or problems within a system, we need to take into account all aspects of that system. In his work on creativity, Csikszentmihalyi (1999) outlined several sets of questions to help researchers identify influences on creativity that operate within the different components of a system, including the cultural context (made up of the domain and the culture it is part of), the social context (made up of the field and its society), and the individual context (made up of the individual and his or her personal background). (To review a visual of the systems model, see Figure 2.1, in Chapter 2.) While these analytic questions are very useful for understanding the roles that different aspects of the system play in innovation, they tend to isolate certain issues to single system components. Accessibility, for example, is tied to domain within this framework (e.g., the accessibility of the discipline's language and specialist knowledge to newcomers, through education, journals, or other means), but in fact issues of accessibility might be relevant at the individual level as well (e.g., the extent to which the individual's personal circumstances—such as geographic or educational location, or personal background—affect his or her abilities to access the information and norms of the discipline).

Another limitation to the systems-based model described in Chapter 2 is its potential for representing systems as closed and stable rather than dynamic, fluid, and complex. Lemke (1993, 1995, 2000) offers the concept of ecosocial systems as an alternative, describing an ecosocial system as "a human social community taken together with the material ecosystem that enables, supports, and constrains it" (Lemke, 1993, p. 262). Key to the distinction Lemke draws between classical systems theory and dynamic, complex systems is the idea that ecosystems are not made up of *things* but of *processes*. Ecosocial systems are also consistent with ecological approaches to language, which view language holistically as shaped by individuals, situations, cultural groups, and social factors. Language can thus be understood as "the complex totality of the speakers' situational positioning and the sociocultural and socioeconomic characteristics of the speech communities" (Kramsch & Steffensen, 2008, p. 18). Viewing genre innovation ecologically and ecosocially helps to emphasize the highly social, material, and interrelated processes involved, as well as the potential for individual acts of innovation to contribute to changes in a community's genres.

In this final section, I lay out a heuristic for exploring some of the ecosocial elements that can shape possibilities for, impediments to, and the nature of innovation in academic genres. Some of these factors are adapted from Csikszentmihalyi's (1999) more general systems-based analysis. I have identified others by drawing on scholarship on academic disciplines and research, including the analytic tools outlined in Chapter 2. Within each area presented, I begin with a list of sample questions that might be used as prompts for researchers, instructors, or students analyzing the possibilities for genre innovation within a given system.

Accessibility and Availability

- How accessible is the discipline and/or local community, including its practices for knowledge construction, to outsiders and newcomers?
- What kinds of resources (subject-matter knowledge, languages, genres, material tools) are needed to gain expertise and insider status within the discipline and/or local community?
- How selective and restrictive is the discipline and/or local community to students and new scholars?

The more barriers to **accessing** the knowledge, norms, and practices of a discipline, the more difficult it becomes to introduce innovation (Csikszentmihalyi, 1999). Highly specialized knowledge, jargon-ridden language, limited space for newcomers, or the use of a *lingua franca,* for example, could all prevent potential innovators from joining a disciplinary community. Similarly, when information and resources within a discipline—such as cutting-edge research, specialized lab equipment, or conference attendance—is restricted, some individuals are prevented from contributing; often, those individuals are more likely to be from underrepresented, marginalized groups. Examining academic publishing, Canagarajah (1996, 2002) has drawn attention to some of the barriers to disciplinary contributions faced by scholars in Periphery countries that lack the resource **availability** that their colleagues in Center countries enjoy. In other words, despite their great potential for offering fresh perspectives and approaches, barriers of access—material and social—can limit the likelihood that such individuals will be able to offer such contributions.

Across academic disciplines and even geographical regions (domestic and global), issues of access and availability will vary. The hard sciences, for instance, are often highly restricted in terms of specialized knowledge and research resources and tools. In many countries, only students who score in the top percentiles of national university exams may enter these fields. Even once students are admitted into science degree programs, they typically face a series of "weed-out" courses, which force many to change their field of study. On the other end of the spectrum are the humanities. Though disciplines like literature, history, and sociology may, in some respects, be more academically accessible to students, they often face other barriers to participation. For instance, in the United States, faculty positions in the humanities and social sciences have become increasingly difficult to obtain, with only approximately one-third of graduates in fields like literature and modern languages securing tenure-track positions (Modern Language Association, 2015)—and without such a position, innovative contributions to the field's discourses and genres become even more difficult. Further, the often highly jargon-ridden discourse of some humanities disciplines may serve as a deterrent to many students who may otherwise have an interest in humanistic study.

Disciplines, of course, are neither monolithic nor homogenous, and local, institutional configurations of disciplinary members can be equally important to processes of genre innovation. Genres are performed not just in the pages of international journals but at national and local conferences, in departmental meetings, in program-based events (like dissertation defenses), and in classrooms. So while a particular discipline might be broadly considered restrictive or exclusionary to all but seasoned members, localized social groups of disciplinary members may enact different values and make available different resources, thereby being more or less accessible to newcomers (and more or less tolerant of difference and innovation). Accessibility and resource availability, then, need to be considered at micro- and macro-level ecologies.

Roles and Hierarchies

- What roles are taken up by the author(s)/researcher(s) and reader(s)? What is the balance of power?
- What kind of cultural or symbolic capital has the author/researcher accumulated in the eyes of those who will evaluate innovation?
- What are the risks of innovation for the author/researcher?
- What kinds of innovation are valued by those with power in the community, and what kinds are discouraged?

In the traditional academic classroom, clearly defined roles of the teacher (as expert and assessor) and the student (as novice and learner) shape how student texts are both written and read, and they limit the likelihood that a student will depart from genre expectations. As an assessor, an instructor is in the position of teaching norms and conventions to students and therefore looks for evidence that students have been successful in this endeavor. School, indeed, is largely a process of learning to carry out genres in preferred ways, and it is the teacher's *role* to facilitate this process. As such, where a peer may judge a norm-breaking text to be innovative, a teacher may judge it to be transgressive because it does not demonstrate the student's ability to adopt the preferred (taught) conventions—though, of course, this process will depend largely on the individual teacher and course. In the *role* of learners, students' practice is also shaped by their position of relatively little power in the classroom. Students, for the most part, know that their role is to demonstrate a "mastery" of knowledge, including knowledge of genre norms, and are in most cases unlikely to stray from that aim. It is typically only the students who have already demonstrated such mastery who are granted the opportunity to innovate.

All this is not to say that opportunities for innovation do not arise in academic classrooms. Many teachers do, for example, give non-traditional assignments or encourage students to experiment with new media in their writing—Thaiss and Zawacki (2006) found that these were generally the same faculty members who themselves engaged in alternative forms of knowledge production, suggesting that their commitment to stretching discursive or generic boundaries was not limited to their scholarship. Yet, while these instructors often assigned creative tasks (such as asking nursing students to write children's stories on being a nurse), they still expected student responses to fall within the expected boundaries of the assignment's genre. As the researchers put it, teachers who offer inventive tasks "have already considered a range of differing student responses that fall within their objectives" (Thaiss & Zawacki, 2006, p. 90). Alternative conceptualizations of an assignment, arrangement of information, or language and dialect usage on the part of students were thus generally discouraged—and students avoided them too, wanting to work within guidelines set by teachers. Originality in content or ideas was considered a more valued (and safer) approach to innovation for these students and faculty, a finding echoed in Allison's (2004) exploration of academic writing and creativity in an EFL setting. In his survey study with teachers in an English language university program in Singapore, Allison found that some teachers distinguished between originality, which they valued, and creativity, which they associated with literary writing and viewed as a negative trait in academic writing.

Although both Allison's (2004) and Thaiss and Zawacki's (2006) studies examine single institutions, they do suggest some shared features of academic classrooms with relation to innovation, namely a preference toward genre conformity on the part of teachers and perhaps students. Other studies have suggested additional constraints that may discourage innovation: dominant language ideologies, *de facto* classroom or program language policies, and students' fear of outcomes can all serve to inhibit student innovation (Allison, 2004; Belcher, 2009; Belcher & Hirvela, 2005; Canagarajah, 2006a; Casanave, 2010). These studies highlight how power differences inherent to classroom structures shape and limit possibilities for student genre innovation.

The institutional and social **hierarchies** of academic research similarly discourage newer and minority scholars from bending genre norms too drastically. Well-developed gatekeeping structures such as grant review boards or journal editorial boards serve to control the range of genre variation that is considered acceptable within a disciplinary domain. In general, these peer reviewers are those who have been in the field for a long time and have demonstrated their expertise (by passing through the very same gatekeeping system). As experts, they have likely worked for years mastering the norms and conventions of their discipline's research genres, and they are therefore often invested in protecting those norms—potentially then limiting the possibilities for genre innovation. Graduate students and junior faculty can gain acceptance in a field only by passing through these gatekeeping structures, a process that has a stabilizing effect on the discipline's genres, encouraging some commitment to conformity.

Passing through the gatekeeping system is also important in accumulating the kind of cultural capital that, as we saw in Chapter 2, can aid in the reception of a text as innovative rather than deviant. Those who are successful in publishing and securing grants accumulate citations to their work, name recognition, and institutional promotion, and eventually are themselves placed in gatekeeping positions. Without the capital that experts enjoy, novices are generally not granted the freedom to bend or flout conventions in the way that experts are. Reflecting on her own publishing journey, Ryuko Kubota (2003) warns that "it is advisable for a writer to follow closely the conventions at least in the initial stages of writing for publication in order to gain the cultural capital that will facilitate her or his initiation into the academic community" (p. 65).

But bending genres is not only about perception and the ways in which increased cultural capital aids in the perception of a norm-bending genre as innovative. It is also about risks—and here newer scholars have much more to lose than those considered to be disciplinary experts. Non-tenured faculty members, for example, are often cautioned against taking risks in their scholarship, whether that be through the topics they study, the methodologies they adopt, or the forms and venues in which they write. Innovation, in any of these areas, is often perceived as threatening one's chance at tenure success or, even worse, blacklisting a young academic from the ivory towers of the profession. There is much at stake for the new scholar trying to break in to a field, and departing from a discipline's norms is often perceived as an unnecessary risk. In other words, it is not simply the case that experts are able to get away with innovations because of their positions of power; it is also the case that they are *more likely* to take on this kind of risk—for them, the risk is simply less risky.

Collaboration

- Is research typically carried out by individuals, pairs, or groups?
- How stratified is collaborative work? (For example, does it take place with a clear leader managing subordinates, or is a more or less equal effort?)

Sociocultural approaches to creativity counter myths of the lone creative genius, working away in a lab or studio in isolation, but research suggests that creativity is instead social and *collaborative* (Sawyer, 2012). Sawyer draws on research of jazz ensembles and improvisation theatre groups to demonstrate the ways in which creativity is derived from the interactions of the group rather than from the contributions of any one individual within the group. Psychologist Kevin Dunbar (1995, 1999) has extensively researched scientific creativity, which his work suggests is similarly distributed, often resulting from research group meetings and discussions. A group—especially one composed of people who bring diverse perspectives—benefits from the generation and discussion of alternative hypotheses and models, an especially important part of scientific research. Dunbar's work offers an important reminder that much academic work is highly social and collaborative in nature. Although I have so far highlighted issues like identity, ethos, and self-expression in relation to genre innovation, it is important to keep in mind that these concepts need not be tied to a single author. Even when they appear so on paper, innovations from single authors are nearly always the outcome of many social interactions and even some kind of co-authorship. At the very least, they are highly influenced by textual encounters.

The emphasis and value placed on collaboration may differ significantly across disciplinary, institutional, and educational contexts, along with the nature of the collaborative interaction itself. In school settings, individuals work together through group tasks and projects, though these often bring with them constraints not present in scholarly collaboration—for example, collaboration may be a requirement, peers may not work effectively together, and the ultimate goal is generally task completion with a strong grade, rather than discovery or advancement of knowledge.

Within academic research, collaboration is particularly common in many science and social science disciplines, with projects sometimes requiring a large number of hands to carry out, if not analyze, the work. In these cases, group efforts may also be marked by hierarchical structures whereby a single person serves as the lab director or primary investigator, while others serve subordinate, often ranked, roles. While such power dynamics do not necessarily impede the kind of innovation possible through collaboration, they differ from more lateral collaborations as found in, for example, jazz ensembles or some joint-authored research.

Novelty and Originality

- To what extent is novelty valued in the discipline?
- How is novelty defined within the discipline? What kind of novelty is valued and considered innovative? What kind is discouraged?
- Are there constraints on who can create novel work, or on what kind of novelty different community members are encouraged or discouraged from?

Novelty and originality, which contribute to innovation, are central to academic research, evidenced by their frequent appearance in criteria for evaluating publication manuscripts, grant proposals, awards and fellowships, student research papers, and even college admission essays. Indeed, academic communities have been characterized as "factories of novelty, encouraging members to plod toward their yearly quota of inspirational leaps" (Kaufer & Geisler, 1989, p. 286). As such, rhetorical appeals to novelty are common in research article abstracts across disciplines and are particularly pervasive in the hard sciences, where stressing novelty is a chief means of claiming a study's significance (Hyland, 2000). But despite some disciplinary differences in how originality and novelty are defined and judged, *newness* is entrenched in academics' views of knowledge production. Academic genres often index this value, emphasizing a work's originality through move structures, persuasive appeals, and linguistic features. On the one hand, then, highlighting novelty is conventional, an expected characteristic of many academic genres; on the other hand, novelty that is unexpected or that pushes conventional boundaries may hold particular persuasive power.

Perhaps because of the expectation in academic research for some new contribution, innovations that strive to offer novel ideas or approaches are not always stark departures from convention. Rather, research that challenges previously held ideas or approaches cannot stand entirely apart from prior scholarship—it must instead work to recognize and represent a field's consensual knowledge base and then question it and move beyond it in some way (Kaufer & Geisler, 1989; Swales & Leeder, 2012). Studying expert (faculty) and novice (student) approaches to research-based writing, for example, Kaufer and Geisler (1989) found that the novices lacked the insider knowledge necessary to represent existing knowledge and then break with consensus; they didn't have, in the researchers' words, "the concept of novelty as a design strategy" (p. 297). Explored from this perspective, then, novelty might be considered a rhetorical strategy but one that is just as likely to be conceptual or ideational as formal or linguistic in nature. In other words, novelty need not be limited to a text's formal structure; it could be found in the choice of research method, the topic, the context of inquiry, or the unique blending of theories or disciplinary scholarship, to name just a few examples.

The alignment of student novelty with originality of ideas rather than with the adoption of new approaches or alternative forms of discourse is also evidenced by writing rubrics, which tend to reward originality of thought but conventionality of form, as in these examples (from California State University, Bakersfield, 2006):

> A 6 paper commands attention because of its **insightful development** and mature style. It presents a cogent analysis of or response to the text, elaborating that response with well-chosen examples and persuasive reasoning. The 6 paper shows that its writer can usually choose words aptly, use sophisticated sentences effectively, and **observe the conventions of written English**. (University of California, Subject A test)

> Thesis/Focus: (a) Originality: Develops **fresh insight** that challenges the reader's thinking; (b) Clarity: Thesis and purpose are clear to the reader; **closely match the writing task**. (Northeastern Illinois University, Writing Rubric)

> Presentation: ...3. **Organization is** purposeful, effective, and **appropriate**; 4. **Sentence form and word choice are varied and appropriate**; 5. **Punctuation, grammar, spelling, and mechanics are appropriate.**

> Thinking: ...11. **Independent thinking** is evident; 12. **Creativity/ originality** is evident. (California State University, Long Beach, Analytical Writing Rubric)

To some extent these value systems simply reflect the overall goal of U.S. education, which emphasizes critical thinking within established genres of communication and practice. Demonstrating control over those genres is crucial in most classroom environments, so that departures from norms are only granted value *after* such a demonstration has been made.

In academic publishing, novelty is more likely to be an explicit value, but even here the nature of that novelty may be only vaguely—if at all—defined. For instance, the next excerpt is taken from the general peer review guidelines for journals published by the large academic publisher Elsevier:

> Originality: Is the article sufficiently novel and interesting to warrant publication? Does it add to the canon of knowledge? Does the article adhere to the journal's standards? Is the research question an important one? In order to determine its originality and appropriateness for the journal, it might be helpful to think of the research in terms of what percentile it is in? Is it in the top 25% of papers in this field? You might wish to do a quick literature search using tools such as Scopus to see if there are any reviews of the area. If the research has been covered previously, pass on references of those works to the editor. (Elsevier, n.d.)

This lack of clarity regarding the nature of novelty or originality has been a concern of Michèle Lamont and her colleagues, who have carried out one of the few empirical studies of perceptions of novelty in academic research. After identifying originality as a major criterion for grant funding, Lamont (2009) examined how grant reviewers from various social science and humanities disciplines define this concept. While research in the sociology of knowledge has identified originality in science as referring to new theories or findings, definitions of originality appear to cover a broader range in the social sciences and humanities, including research topic, theory, method, data, results, approach or perspective, and geographical area or time period studied (Guetzkow, Lamont, & Mallard, 2004) Most common of these defi nitions among the 71 funding reviewers interviewed for Guetzkow, Lamont, & Mallard's (2004) study[1] were original approach and original theory; the least common was original results. Though an emphasis on originality of results may be partially expected in a funding competition, in which results have yet to be obtained, the researchers still note

---

[1] Definitions of originality were derived from interviewees' discussion of research proposals, when the research was referred to as *original, novel, innovative, new,* or *doing something others have not* (Guetzkow, Lamont, & Mallard, 2004).

that the emphasis on "making a new discovery" seems to be of less importance in the social sciences and humanities in comparison with the natural sciences.

Guetzkow, Lamont, and Mallard's (2004) study delves further into perceptions of originality by comparing reviewers' definitions and descriptions across disciplines. A cross-disciplinary comparison showed that those in the humanities and history most commonly referred to originality in terms of approach while those in the social sciences most commonly defined originality in terms of method. Additionally, originality of forms of data was much more common in the humanities than other areas, and social scientists appear to have the broadest range of definitions of originality, giving relatively equal emphasis to originality in approach, topic, and theory. In the end, the researchers argue that these distinctions are linked to disciplinary rhetorics or epistemic cultures—in short, different approaches to and values regarding knowledge construction.

In addition to demonstrating that perceptions of novelty—or, by extension, innovation—may vary by discipline, Guetzkow, Lamont, & Mallard's (2004) work also sheds light on some of "non-substantive" influences on these perceptions—specifically, reviewers' perceptions of a researcher's moral qualities. When a proposal was judged to be original, reviewers very often described its author in morally positive terms, such as "adventurous, ambitious, bold, courageous, curious, independent, intellectually honest, and risk taking… 'challenging the status quo,' thinking for themselves' and 'having a passion for ideas'" (p. 203). In contrast, the authors of proposals viewed as unoriginal were described as "conformist, complacent, derivative, facile, gap-filling, hackneyed, lazy, parochial, pedestrian, rehashing, tired, traditional, uncritical…'riding on the bandwagon,' or 'throwing around buzz words'" (p. 203). This analysis suggests the importance of ethos-building in perceptions of innovation—a connection drawn out previously in Chapter 2.

Heterogeneity, Mobility, and Globalization

- How diverse are the members of the discipline and/or local community of users in areas like culture, ethnicity/race, gender, language, etc.? How diverse are the gatekeepers and others who hold high status in the discipline?

- To what extent do the discipline and/or local community (including the gatekeepers) engage with other disciplines? To what degree is it influenced by other disciplines? How accepting are the gatekeepers of interdisciplinary perspectives and approaches?

- How much mobility (global, disciplinary, social) is there within the discipline and/or local community?

- How globalized is the discipline and/or the local community?

As Becher and Trowler's (2001) work demonstrates, similarities within disciplinary communities may be expected on some level, but such communities are also characterized by diversity, and such diversity plays out on local and global scales. Interaction among diverse people and approaches, for instance, can create synergistic environments and collaborations that give rise to new ideas and practices. There is also some evidence that domains and their gatekeeping groups that include members with diverse backgrounds and approaches may be more accepting of innovation (Csikszentmihalyi, 1999)—perhaps because of their exposure or openness to divergent ways of thinking and doing. Gatekeepers in relatively homogeneous disciplinary communities, for example, may be less likely to judge genre departures as innovative (or positive) compared with more *heterogeneous* gatekeeping groups.

Of course, characterizing the diversity of a community is a complicated issue in and of itself, partially because diversity is indexed through such a wide range of scales and partially because it is difficult to quantify. A discipline like chemistry, for instance, is on the one hand dominated by male scholars (likely from similar socioeconomic backgrounds) but is, internationally, made up of individuals with a broad range of linguistic, ethnic, and cultural backgrounds. But diversity also plays out within localized academic communities: a university department, a group of university student majors, a national journal, and an international professional organization may all demonstrate diversity (or homogeneity) to differing degrees. Further, characteristics of diversity may vary between wider social groups and the decision-making gatekeepers of a discipline, who often yield more power in facilitating (or limiting) genre innovation. For instance, a journal editorial board or grant review board that is made up primarily of people trained through a single program or disciplinary paradigm may be less likely to find alternative, divergent approaches acceptable (or innovative), thereby excluding them from the larger domain.

Increases in university student diversity have recently also become an interest of writing studies scholars, who have argued in favor of giving voice to marginalized student writers by inviting new forms, styles, and ways of knowing into more traditional academic discourse. Such work has most commonly attended to contexts such as undergraduate writing in English-dominant countries (e.g., Ivanič, 1998; Schroeder, Fox, & Bizzell, 2002; Smitherman & Villanueva, 2003) and graduate student thesis and dissertation writing (e.g., Casanave, 2010; Phan Le Ha, 2009). Noting that strict adherence to a dominant discourse has an exclusionary and homogenizing effect, many writing studies scholars have sought to affirm the potential of non-traditional discourses for bringing new perspectives into the academy. Given the growing diversity of universities and the globalization of academic scholarship, this work seeks to open up the linguistic marketplace or at least encourage (among students and teachers) a critical meta-awareness of the power dynamics at play in academic writing. Though the primary focus of this work has been on the writing classroom, a systems-based orientation suggests that as much (or more) attention might be given to raising the awareness of faculty in other disciplines about diverse and alternative discourses.

Increased migration and *globalization* has affected not just local student populations but also the more general nature of academe and academic communication. To some extent, academic research has always been international, with scholars moving around the globe for academic study, research sabbaticals, collaborations, professional meetings, and invited lectures. But the current globalization of higher education and scholarly research more broadly is in many ways unique, reflecting the broader waves of global migration that characterize this century (Hamilton & Pitt, 2009; Horner et al., 2011). On the one hand, unprecedented numbers of students and faculty are studying or teaching outside of their home countries (Institute of International Education, 2011); in addition, many universities have established "off-shore" or "branch" campuses in other countries, so that a student in Oman, for example, may attend and receive a degree from a British or U.S. university without leaving home. Concurrently, the dynamics of academic publication have changed rather dramatically over the past few decades, with more widely available online access to academic journals, a strong trend toward the overwhelming use of English as the language of publication, and increasing pressure in many countries to publish in highly ranked "international" (nearly always Anglophone) journals. Combined, these trends point to higher mobility of people and resources and a greater reliance on the English language as at least one means of communication within academic communities.

Since the 1980s, applied linguists have followed these changes and considered the implications for academic genres like research articles (e.g., Baldauf & Jernudd, 1983a, 1983b; Swales, 1985, 1997). Despite speculation that the traditional English language research article (RA) *will* change in response to the growing international diversity of the writers (Swales, 2004)—even arguments that it *must* change (Belcher, 2007; Canagarajah, 2002)—little research has specifically examined these changes or, more importantly for this discussion, the possibilities for innovation within this global publishing context. Deviation from traditional norms seems increasingly likely when a genre is being accessed and reproduced by scholars around the globe, who come to the task with varying linguistic, rhetorical, and cultural histories, experiences, and expectations. Rozycki and Johnson's (2013) study examined the presence of "non-canonical" grammar in 14 Best Paper award winners in an international engineering journal. The authors conclude that the field has "organically grown a language that allows all language speakers to communicate with success" (p. 166), and this process plays out through interactions within a dynamic and heterogeneous community. Centripetal forces like peer review and editorial directives act in tandem with the centrifugal, stratifying forces of global diversity. In a reflection of their own copyediting practices, for example, Heng Hartse and Kubota (2014) note that despite their goal of preserving authors' language—including non-dominant features of lexico-grammar—they were often unable to do so in practice due to the complex social and political environment in which academic writing and publishing occurs.

Within this push-and-pull environment, some unconventional texts are likely to be discarded as *too* different, and a range of reasons will inform those judgments; yet some texts will be accepted, identified as innovative, and eventually enter into the discourse of the field. The process of change may be slow, but we are doubtless at a point in time in which the process is at work and may indeed be visible to the analyst who wishes to examine it. Fields that are more fully internationalized (i.e., in which top journals have international editorial boards, annual meetings are held around the world, and cross-country or cross-continental collaborations are common) may be more ripe for and accepting of academic genre innovation. On the other hand, such fields may implement stricter control of genre conventions in order to maintain stability and uniformity in the face of high levels of cultural and linguistic variation.

Resources for Innovations

- What kinds of resources are available for innovation, including technologies, languages, material spaces, and social contexts?
- To what extent do available resources encourage or facilitate innovation?
- To what extent are these resources valued and encouraged?

While innovation does not always require particular *resources,* some resources may aid in the development of innovative work. New technologies, for example, can give a fresh spin to traditional conventions of practices and products, as in the examples of citizen science described earlier in this chapter. Currently, technology is being used to challenge conventional practices of peer review, a central feature of many academic research genres. In open source or crowd-sourced peer review, a manuscript is posted in an online space for a short time and made available for review by a large number of readers (either editorial board members or any readers who wish to partici-pate). The practice itself is innovative in the sense that it departs from norms (though some may view it as a problematic departure), but it may also support the emergence of innovative research and/or forms of research dissemination. When the gatekeepers are no longer a small, hand-picked group of disciplinary members, they are likely to repre-sent a wider swath of the discipline, some possibly more willing to admit new approaches and forms into the disciplinary domain.

New technologies are also being picked up to challenge traditional forms of many academic research genres. A survey by the Modern Language Association of 1,330 humanities departments in the United States, for example, demonstrated that, as of 2006, 10 percent of the dissertations in these departments were digital (Jaschik, 2012). An increasing number of online journals that present work through hyper-text or other non-linear, non-traditional forms are also available. These alternative mediums for sharing research are still not entirely accepted by tenure and promotion review boards (Modern Language Associa-tion, 2006), demonstrating the challenge these kinds of genre innova-tions face in their reception. In the sciences, technology similarly aids in the development of innovative change to research genres, as authors strive to find ways to incorporate animation, high-resolution visuals, or other forms of data presentation into their work; journals, for exam-ple, increasingly allow for the addition of online content that cannot be produced in printed pages.

Aside from technology, other resources exist within disciplinary groups that may aid in the production of innovative genres. In some disciplinary groups, language can serve as a key resource for innova-tion, giving researchers access to a wide range of information, to key populations of study, or to social-professional networks. Language can also be used creatively within research genres, bending traditional pat-terns of form. Other resources for innovation might include material spaces (such as labs, meeting places, or libraries) or social contexts (which give rise to collaborations and brainstorming that can generate innovative ideas).

Access to and value of these kinds of resources for innovation may vary considerably not only by institution and discipline but also by classroom. In some classroom contexts, for instance, students may have access to computers with an array of software and hardware tools and with tutorial support for learning and using these tools. In other environments, resources may be low-tech but high in linguistic or other resources that aid in creativity. The value of such resources will also vary by classroom context, influenced by assessment standards and educational policies, among other things.

Genre

> - How long is the genre's history?
> - What is at stake with the genre?
> - How many levels of control or gatekeeping might influence the genre's final form?
> - Who are the genre's gatekeepers, and what is their hierarchical relationship to the genre's author(s)?
> - How difficult is the genre to learn? Is it formally taught through instruction or guidelines?

In an academic research environment, numerous *genres* coalesce and coordinate to produce and share knowledge, ranging from short conference program abstracts to fellowship application letters, faculty biostatements, to lab reports, research articles, and senior thesis projects. While some genres may be relatively open to innovation, even for the author on the low end of the proverbial totem pole, others seem more resistant to variation and norm-departing—Bhatia's (2006) characterization of genres as "liberal" or "conservative" in this respect is particularly useful. In other words, genres are not equal in their innovation potential.

Genre theory has shown us that all genres change, but often change is more rapid in a genre's nascent days. Genres supported through new technologies often demonstrate this kind of early instability, as Miller and Shepherd (2004) demonstrate in their discussion of web logs, or "blogs." One newly emerging research genre is the video abstract, available on some publishers' websites and also increasingly displayed on webpages of research lab groups to give a short video introduction to their work. The videos currently vary considerably, with some focusing just on a close-up of one researcher's face as he or she explains the project, others incorporating animated visuals to illustrate the details of the work, and still others featuring a quick mini-lesson on the chalkboard. As the video abstract ages, however, we are likely to see norms emerge, certainly with regard to content and form, but possibly also in relation to camera angle, the researcher's attire, and the surrounding environment or backdrop. Video abstracts in business-related fields already utilize high-quality production technologies and are visibly more sophisticated (and expensive) to produce than those typically found in the social sciences, presumably influenced by the financial resources available to researchers and perhaps by institutional support.

What this example suggests is that the video abstract as a genre currently offers a relatively strong contrast to the scientific research article in terms of innovation potential. At this point in time, the genre lacks the history and the norms and expectations that accompany that history, giving authors much more freedom in their approach as users collaboratively work to identify the social actions that the genre can perform and how it might best do so. In contrast, innovation in a more stabilized(-for-now) genre with a long history may be a bit more clear-cut to users: the norms are established and so too are the departures from those norms. It may be the case that the ideal genre for innovation is one that has already acquired some norms but has not yet become so fixed as to be considered almost sacred and unchangeable to its users. On the other hand, innovation is more likely to be noteworthy in established genres.

In addition to having different histories, genres have different futures or outcomes riding on them. Innovating in high-stakes genres like a tenure/promotion review report, multimillion-dollar grant proposal, or TOEFL®'s writing exam carries risk, so authors are more likely to play it safe and adhere to at least most of the expectations. Effective innovations in these situations may be more subtle and less challenging of the status quo, and they may center on innovative content or ideas more than innovative form. But there are also academic genres that carry much lower stakes, such as acknowledgments, faculty webpages, or student assignments that make up only a small portion of a course grade. Here, authors may feel more freedom to take ownership over the genre and bend conventions in ways that meet the author's goals.

Lower-stakes genres are also often less regulated by gatekeeping structures or may be judged by peers or colleagues who wield less power over the author and the genre. In general, it seems to be the case that heavily regulated genres (i.e., those with strong gatekeeping mechanisms) are more resistant to innovations than those that undergo less evaluation. Consider, for example, a proposal for research funding from a national agency. In most cases, before a grant even reaches the review board, it receives an indication of interest from the program officer and a review and endorsement from the researcher's home university—the agency's review board may then have multiple levels of review (Tardy, 2003). Academic research articles similarly undergo numerous influences along the way, often read by peers prior to submission, journal editors who determine whether or not the manuscript will be reviewed, two or three reviewers (or possibly more if the manuscript goes through multiple rounds of review), proofreaders, and copyeditors (Burrough-Boenisch, 2003; Li, 2007). At each stage, convention-flouting is likely to be detected and may be dismissed as inappropriate for the journal. Burrough-Boenisch (2003) refers to these outside influences as "shapers," which seems an appropriate label given their potential to shape the text to conform to a norm.

The gatekeepers themselves may also influence the likelihood that a norm-departing genre will be judged as innovative, though not necessarily in predictable ways. Gatekeepers with a long history of experience in the discipline tend to agree on which norm-departures are "creative" or "innovative" and which are problematic or inappropriate

(Sawyer, 2012). Similarly, we might expect that a relatively homogenous group of gatekeepers would share views on innovation, while a more diverse group may be more open to new approaches (or at least some members of the group may be). The gatekeepers' status relative to the author or researcher may also be influential: Journal manuscript reviewers may judge norm-departing graduate student papers somewhat harshly while graduate student conference organizers may be quite open to accepting innovative conference papers. The situation is further complicated by the roles and expectations that gatekeepers play, even when they support innovative and resistant approaches. In a reflective dialogue on one new scholar's publishing experience at *TESOL Quarterly*, Suresh Canagarajah and Ena Lee (2014) demonstrate that even a sympathetic editor is usually committed to some dominant values of publishing, such as how one appropriately enters and contributes to a conversation. While Lee (the author) wanted to resist dominant discourses, Canagarajah (the journal editor) felt that her work had to engage with those discourses more closely. He reflects that "although I valued hybridity, there are different levels and extents of discoursal merger; Ena's approach kept dissimilar discourses too far apart rather than merging them seamlessly" (pp. 71–72).

Finally, the genre's difficulty to learn and master could play a role in the production and acceptance of innovation. Conference paper proposals or author biostatements are research genres that can be grasped fairly easily from examining a few typical samples. Research articles or student research papers, on the other hand, generally pose a much greater challenge. Because facility with these genres requires complex genre knowledge, they can take years to learn and control adeptly. Meta-genres such as books and websites exist to instruct learners in the conventions of the genres, and many receive instruction through formal coursework, tutorials, or mentoring to support their learning. Given the lengthy and often arduous process of learning the conventions of these genres—and given the clear visibility of conventions that must be learned—authors may feel invested in maintaining the norms that they worked hard to master.

As this discussion has shown, innovation in academic research genres is not uniform across genres; instead, many aspects of the genre itself—its history, its present currency or value—play a central role in the processes of producing and judging innovation. To take this role into account, genre lies at the heart of the possibilities for, constraints against, and acceptance of innovation in academic research and writing.

What I hope emerges from discussions throughout this chapter is a picture of a highly complex, contingent, and interactive ecosocial system of academic writing and research. Within such an environment, the success of any given instance of genre innovation is not predictable but instead shaped within social and material environments. For instance, the description of a radical methodology in a grant proposal or the incorporation of informal language into a research article may be successful in one instance yet unsuccessful in another. The specific discipline, the gatekeepers, the individual author, the genre, and the circumstances of production and reception will all coordinate to ultimately shape the acceptance or rejection of norm-departing practices. What this perspective lacks in predictability, however, it compensates for in heuristic power. For authors, gatekeepers, learners, and genre researchers, an ecological system perspective presents an analytic framework that can help illuminate where possibilities and obstacles to innovation may exist. Awareness of such obstacles can, at the very least, offer a first step toward system transformation.

Chapter 4

Convention and Innovation in Learning (to Write in) a Discipline

"Creativity doesn't come in the flowery language if you're writing a research paper. Creativity comes in the great thinking, the creative thinking that you do when you come up with your project in the first place, when you interpret your data, and when you think about where you can take it. And that's hard work."

—*Environmental science course professor*

Much of my interest in genre innovation has been prompted by my curiosity about writing in the academic disciplines, particularly within STEM (science, technology, engineering, and mathematics) fields. In my experience, writing and language instructors and students tend to construct these fields—including their approaches to research and their written communication of that research—as more rigid and conventional than the social sciences or humanities and therefore often assume that creativity and innovation have less of a role for learners in these disciplines, especially in terms of their writing. Studying innovation in science research genres would, I thought, be an interesting challenge, especially in the context of an undergraduate classroom where students would presumably be striving to learn conventional norms rather than to exploit those norms. In the spring of 2011, I spent 10 weeks observing an advanced undergraduate research course in environmental science, beginning with a fairly simple question: *How are creativity and innovation constructed and valued within the process of introducing students to disciplinary writing and research?*

95

Many readers will be familiar with the robust body of scholarship that has examined disciplinary research writing classrooms at the undergraduate level. Studies by Herrington (1985, 1988) and Wilder (2002), for example, examined the functions of writing within different disciplines and the ways in which disciplinary values for knowledge construction are conveyed within classroom environments. According to Herrington (1985), writing in classroom communities carries out multiple functions, introducing students to the intellectual, formal, and social activities and roles of a discipline. Though Herrington and others do acknowledge the heterogeneity and locality of disciplinary classrooms, Prior (1998) argues for an orientation that adopts an even greater recognition of such complexity. Disciplines should be viewed, he suggests, as "open networks, forged through relational activity that intermingles personal, interpersonal, institutional, and sociocultural histories" (p. 25). This view is important for understanding genre in the classroom, as it turns attention to both the centrifugal and centripetal forces acting upon language; it also aligns well with the ecological orientation to understanding innovation outlined in Chapter 3.

A related thread of research has examined the disciplinary writing of experts by exploring published academic writing. Many studies in this area have focused on textual distinctions across disciplines, examining areas such as lexico-grammatical conventions, rhetorical structures, and citation use, and ultimately providing ample evidence of cross-disciplinary variation. Most noteworthy are studies like those by Hyland (2000) that link discourse conventions to larger disciplinary values and practices. Research into disciplinary rhetorical practices has also brought much light into the ways in which disciplinary genres embed particular ideologies, identities, and beliefs (Bazerman, 1988; Hyland, 2000; Kaufer & Geisler, 1989). For the most part, studies of published disciplinary writing have focused their attention on the enactment of convention within disciplinary communities rather than on in-group variation, though there are important exceptions. Swales' (1998) textography of the three floors of one university building offers a picture of discourse community as varied, fluid, personal, dialogic, and layered—a view that very much aligns with that of Prior's (1998), though Swales does not adopt the sociohistorical activity theory lens that underlies Prior's work. As discussed in Chapter 2, Hyland (2008,

2010) has also studied the ways in which the writing of individuals may break from community norms, but he has focused specifically on high-status disciplinary experts who have already built up the capital that grants them a profit of distinction and the right to write in unconventional ways (Bourdieu, 1991).

As this brief discussion suggests, research of disciplinary writing and learning has not ignored variation or innovation, and most studies have acknowledged that disciplinarity is not homogenous. At the same time, a great deal of research in this area has taken convention as the key focus, with less explicit study of innovation overall. This focus is not surprising. Learning and performing convention is, after all, essential to disciplinary participation and success, as it helps to bring coherence to the diverse practices and values that make up a community of practice. Taking research on disciplinary genre practice as a starting point, what might we learn by exploring the role of innovation or the centrifugal forces in academic genres, particularly in the experiences of novice writers and those who are just beginning to learn disciplinary practices?

In this chapter, I share my research of an undergraduate course that aimed to prepare environmental science majors to do primary research in their field. Within this instructional context, where the learning of privileged disciplinary practice was an important aim, I explore the role of creativity and innovation—*How were they were constructed, valued, and taught by both teacher and students? What are some of the constraints and opportunities that influence creativity and innovation in the classroom?* I begin with a general narrative of the class and then move on to apply the theoretical concepts and frameworks from Chapters 2 and 3 as way to further understand genre innovation and creativity within the classroom site.

Environmental Science and ES 350: Research Methods

As a discipline, environmental science encompasses numerous fields of study, such as soil and wetland science, restoration and urban ecology, or atmospheric science, to name just a few. Research often takes place in natural (including urban) environments as well as in greenhouses and laboratories. The course that I observed, ES 350: Research

Methods, was situated within an environmental science and studies department at a university located in a major metropolis in the United States; many of the program faculty had interests in urban-related issues and adopted interdisciplinary approaches to their study of the environment.

At the time of my study, Research Methods had recently been revised to become a required course in which students would complete a formal proposal for their obligatory senior thesis project. The course was designed to introduce students to scientific research methods and to provide them the time and guidance to begin developing their own research. More specifically, as the course professor described it to me, the primary goal was "to launch them on their thesis," a project they would undertake in their next, and final, year in the program. The Research Methods syllabus stated:

> We will read material on the nature and philosophy of science, experimental design, statistical analysis and scientific writing, focusing on common concerns and pitfalls of the environmental science researcher. Students will build a literature base on a topic to be determined in the first weeks of the course. Students will lead a discussion on a research article from their literature review and over the duration of the course, they will write a research proposal for their senior thesis project. Each proposal will be read by the course instructor and an additional faculty member of the student's choosing, preferably the faculty member who will supervise the senior thesis research. (Research Methods syllabus)

During the first few weeks of the ten-week term, faculty members from the environment science program visited class and described their research interests and projects with the students, who were invited to contact the professors if they would like to work with them, either joining the professor's research team or working on the student's own project under the professor's advisement and guidance. During these first few weeks and throughout the term, students also read several articles about the practices of scientific research, including models of scientific thinking and methods, scientific values, and fraud and ethics in science.

Early in the third week, students submitted a research statement, identifying their research area and possible question(s) for their senior projects. Shortly after this, they began preparing an annotated bibliography, summarizing two articles related to their project every week. At about the same time in the term, two students per class period presented a reading related to their own projects. These articles were distributed in the prior class, and all students were expected to read the selected articles. The student who had chosen the article began by briefly summarizing the reading and its importance, and this was followed by a group discussion of the design, methods, and possible future directions. By the sixth week of the term, students had submitted an initial draft of their research proposal introduction, on which they received feedback from the course instructor. They submitted a penultimate draft of the entire proposal to the instructor and their research advisor by Week 10, and then met with the instructor and advisor for feedback. The final proposal was submitted the following week at the completion of the term. Though the title of the course was Research Methods, it might be best described as a class on *becoming* a scientist, as it introduced students to not just the methods but also the habits of mind of their discipline.

The instructor of Research Methods was a senior faculty member in the environmental science program, whom I refer to as Professor Hanson. (All names in this chapter are pseudonymns.) She was enthusiastic about revising the course to meet its new aims, and her passion for science and science education shone through in her discussions with the students and her interviews with me. In one class discussion, she remarked, "I love doing science, and I'm amazed that I get paid to do science" (Fieldnotes, 31 March 2011). Professor Hanson's investment in designing and teaching the course was evident in both interviews I carried out with her; in our end-of-term interview, for example, she reflected on possible ways to revise the course next year and on aspects she felt she could have taught better.

During the ten-week term, Research Methods met twice per week in a newly constructed science building, the "greenest" building on the urban campus. In each session, the 13 students, Professor Hanson, and I sat around an oblong table in a seminar room with a small whiteboard standing in the corner. The majority of students were about one year from graduation, though a few were a bit closer. While some had already been engaged in scientific research as undergraduate research assistants or as members of research teams, most were embarking on independent research for the first time. Their chosen projects reflected the diversity of approaches found among the faculty members in the department, including topics like the effects of an invasive species on urban biodiversity, the relationship between college students' environmental knowledge and attitude and their ecological behavior patterns, and the development of a taxonomy of shark fossils in the midwestern United States. All 13 students identified English as their dominant language, although two were bilingual in other languages as well. Ten of the 13 students were women, as was typical of the environmental science student population at the university where the study was carried out.

As a researcher, my goal was to understand how creativity and innovation might be discussed, taught, valued, and evaluated in an undergraduate research methods class. The specific questions that guided my study were:

1. How are innovation and creativity in science research writing described and presented to students in an undergraduate science course?

2. How is students' research writing perceived and judged by the course instructor in terms of innovation and creativity?

3. What are some of the constraints and opportunities that influence the processes of genre innovation and creativity in the classroom context?

As an outsider to both the discipline and the course, I took a wide-angle approach to data collection, gathering as much as I could given my own time constraints and my desire to not be too invasive of the professor's time. I attended each of the 20 class sessions, taking fieldnotes and making audio recordings of relevant discussions for later transcription, interviewed the instructor at the beginning and end of the course, collected student writing from 11 of the 13 students, interviewed 5 students after they had submitted their final proposal, and collected all course materials and readings. Through interpretive and reiterative coding, I worked with a research assistant to individually identify dominant themes related to my research questions, to develop and apply coding categories and subcategories, and to refine and re-apply those categories where necessary. The research both challenged and broadened my understanding of genre innovation.

Communicating Values of Creativity and Innovation in Research Methods

Although I understand creativity to be one aspect of innovation, the two were largely conflated in the Research Methods class, and Professor Hanson generally referred to creativity or creative work to encompass the notion of innovation; therefore, I will largely adopt her language in this chapter as well. As discussed in Chapter 2, a sociocultural orientation to creativity broadly characterizes creativity as a product, process, or idea that is considered to be both novel/ original and appropriate/useful by expert community members. One key aspect of this definition is the reliance on judgments from members of the field in perceiving an object or idea positively (as creative) or negatively (as deviant). I did not presume that Professor Hanson would adopt this precise understanding of creativity, so I wanted to gain insight into how she interpreted creativity in relation to science research and research writing. Her own interpretation was important because I assumed that, at least to some extent, she would apply it in her judgments of students' work as innovative and creative or perhaps inappropriate or underprepared.

Through the course readings, classroom discussions, and instructor interviews, I identified two broad themes in Professor Hanson's descriptions and presentations of creativity within the course: The first concerned creative thinking and the second focused on creative expression. As the chapter-opening quotation suggests, Professor Hanson placed more emphasis on the former than the latter.

Creative Thinking

Professor Hanson's discussions of creativity in the Research Methods classroom and in her two interviews with me both reflect the high value she placed on creative thinking in science; to some extent, course readings reinforced this value as well. She described creative thinking as a positive attribute and as part of "doing" good science. At times, her descriptions of such thinking mirrored the sociocultural definition of creativity as novel/original and appropriate/useful, as this classroom exchange illustrates:

> *Prof. Hanson (PH):* What makes something worthy of publishing? When does your research— when does what you're doing through your research here, do you think, become worthy of publishing versus going in a file someplace as your senior thesis?
>
> *Jaclyn:* It's applicable.
>
> *PH:* OK, it's applicable. Applicable to what?
>
> *Jaclyn:* To any other research, or interesting to somebody besides yourself.
>
> *PH:* Yeah, good, so it's of value to somebody else, right? Good. Anybody want to add to that?
>
> *Kurt:* Is it also when it hasn't really been written about?
>
> *PH:* OK. It's original, good. **It's a novel thought, it's original, it contributes to the field, and it's of interest to somebody else.** I don't know that I could say that any better. (Classroom transcript, 14 April 2011, added boldface)

This emphasis on novelty or originality came up in the class throughout the term, often in conjunction with discussions of logic or ideas. For instance, when one student commented that science was a combination of logic and mystery, Professor Hanson said, "I think of it as logic and creativity" (Fieldnotes, 5 April 2011). In commenting to me on the students' final research proposals from the course, Professor Hanson identified creativity as coming through in "original thinking," "a completely novel question," "bringing in something that they didn't—people didn't know it was a gap of knowledge," and being open to multiple outcomes of the research (Interview #2). One of the first assigned class readings encouraged students to use a method of "strong inference" as an alternative way of thinking: devising alternative hypotheses, devising a crucial experiment, carrying it out, and refining remaining possibilities (Platt, 1964). The first two of these steps were described by the author as requiring "intellectual inventions" (p. 347), and the practice of having multiple hypotheses was emphasized by Professor Hanson many times throughout the course. She encouraged students to not be wed to a single hypothesis and to devise experiments in which any outcome would be intriguing. When students demonstrated such thinking in class discussions, they were often met with praise from Professor Hanson through comments like, "That's a creative mind at work right there!" (Fieldnotes, 19 April 2011).

Aware that students aren't always themselves involved in devising the questions or hypothesis that they explore in their work, Professor Hanson acknowledged that they can demonstrate creative thought in other ways, such as how they think through the literature (Fieldnotes, 12 April 2011) or address a research question:

> . . . any other faculty member can give a student a very creative project, and if the student sees how it fits in, then I'm impressed. You know, if they make that story, and they describe a series of experiments that would help them answer the question, even if they didn't come up with the question, I see that as a great product. And yet they didn't come up with the creativity—you know, the idea. (Interview #2)

Creativity, then, was described as coming through in "the design, identifying the question, the interpretation of the data" (Interview

#2)—that is, in the *practice or process* of research rather than the textual product. Professor Hanson modeled and encouraged such thinking regularly in class when students discussed primary research articles in their areas. After students presented an article from their own research area, for example, she would typically ask the others in class to consider follow-up or alternative research designs to what was presented in the article. Often, the students' ideas were met with enthusiastic responses from Professor Hanson, such as "Great idea! I can't believe how creative you guys are" or "Cool idea. That's novel!" (Fieldnotes, 28 April 2011), encouraging them to be innovative in their research designs. In one interview with me, she noted specifically being "impressed with creative ideas that let you design . . . good experiments" (Interview #2). This view of scientific creativity resonates with research by psychologists as well, which describes creative scientists as engaging in problem solving, as well as "ask[ing] good questions and . . . formulat[ing] good problems" (Sawyer, 2012, p. 375).

Creative Expression

While course readings and class discussions did occasionally address creative expression in scientific research writing, the instructor did not emphasize this kind of creativity in class or in her discussion of science writing in our interviews. Rather, it seemed to me that her reaction to this non-traditional expression was more ambivalent. She did not discourage students from adopting less conventional writing styles in their proposals, but she shared her personal preference for more traditional styles and adherence to convention.

Steeped in histories and traditions, science writing is not commonly thought of as a realm for playing with convention, at least not in terms of form (Bazerman, 1988). Within the Research Methods course, writing structure and formatting were generally not presented as having fluid or bendable conventions either. Rather, students were given templates for writing research statements and the various sections of the proposal. Particular attention was given in class to introduction sections, which Professor Hanson described as "all work[ing] the same way—like an inverted triangle" (Classroom transcript, 28 April 2011). She encouraged students to look at the research articles from class as good models to follow for their own introductions, though in reflecting on their final proposals with me, she noted feeling that many of the students needed more guidance in adhering to conventions. She explained, "I had certain expectations and I was surprised and realized that they needed more help in getting to where I wanted them to be" (Interview #2). She described expecting certain rhetorical patterns in their proposals and stated that the next time she teaches the class she would consider "giv[ing] them more guidance on how to organize it" (Interview #1), going beyond just asking students to look at examples as models and assuming that they would be able to adopt these structures in their own writing.

Although writing structure was not presented as a place for creative expression, Professor Hanson did directly address in class conventions of science writing that she felt were changing, including increased use of active voice, present tense, and first person. She told students, "I give you permission" to use these features (Classroom transcript, 5 May 2011). Yet, she did not equate the use of such features with creative language, stating explicitly in class:

> Some journals insist on passive and third person, but journals are becoming more open now. And, not that that lets you put in more creativity, but it makes the writing less cumbersome, and when the writing's less cumbersome, it's less boring. (Classroom transcript, 5 May 2011).

Indeed, the issue of not writing in a "boring" style *did* come up in class, with Professor Hanson repeatedly encouraging students in this regard.

One particularly interesting classroom discussion was sparked by a tongue-in-cheek reading assigned by Professor Hanson, titled "How to Write Consistently Boring Scientific Literature" (Sand-Jensen, 2007). The text outlined ten guidelines "for boring scientific writing" (p. 723), such as "Write long contributions" (p. 724) and "Use many abbreviations and technical terms" (p. 725). In discussing one of the suggestions—"Avoid originality and personality" (p. 724)—Professor Hanson emphasized that students should "tell the reader what you found, what makes it interesting, what makes it different" (Classroom transcript, 5 May 2011), echoing the value she placed on originality and usefulness.

Much more disagreement, however, was generated by the reading's sarcastic suggestion to "Suppress humor and flowery language" (p. 726). Some students admitted to struggling with how to articulate the true, intended recommendation of the author here (was it to use humor and flowery language, they wondered), and Professor Hanson responded, "It's OK to put yourself in your paper. It's OK to be in the paper in some kind of form. It helps—I don't know, I mean I think it helps make not a boring paper, right? But there's a balance there" (Classroom transcript, 5 May 2011). She and one student, Kurt, engaged in a debate about the extent to which using synonyms to make the writing more interesting—rather than using the same terminology over and over throughout the paper—would be appropriate, with Kurt feeling that it might be useful and Professor Hanson being more reluctant:

> Kurt: I think that, a *person* is writing this paper, so giving
>   a personality is OK, but I just think that if you give it
>   personality or you add language that would be, like,
>   your own versus like cookie-cutter science writing, it's
>   gonna help people be more interested and more a part
>   of it. They can see where you're coming from. Because if
>   you say *feline* for cat, I'm pretty sure most people who are
>   reading are gonna know what a feline is versus a cat.
>
> PH: Well, I think that what they were saying before is that,
>   you know, when you're writing, you don't wanna see the
>   same word several times in the sentence so you try to find
>   different words that mean the same thing, so that you're
>   not always using the same word. But in this case, you'd
>   wanna use the same word because you don't wanna
>   confuse the reader.
>
> Kurt: I mean, because, like for me, if it's like "hyperdontic
>   shark," like I see "hyperdontic shark" like every other
>   sentence, but I feel like *cat* is a more basic word that
>   people understand, I don't think that that's a flowery, I
>   feel like that's just [?].

PH: So, you would use different words for a cat, would you?

Kurt: Yeah, I mean if someone tells me not to do it in scientific writing, then I wouldn't because that's the model, [and] then it should be followed. But I feel like that should be broken down if it sounds better. Because if I see *cat* five times in a paragraph, I get bored—at least I get bored when I'm writing *cat* every single, like, couple sentences.

PH: I would say, though, that if you try writing your organism in different ways, you're going to confuse your reader. So that's what you need to balance. I'm not saying one way is—just keep your reader in mind. (Classroom transcript, 5 May 2011)

In the end, Professor Hanson suggested the use of first person instead of interesting synonyms as a strategy for making writing more interest to readers. As she stated, "It [first-person] puts you in without creating text that has personality." The discussion of this particular issue reflected Hanson's more general statement that "Creativity doesn't come in the flowery language if you're writing a research paper" but rather in the innovative scientific thinking.

Hanson's preference for convention over innovation in written expression is not surprising, and I did not view it negatively but rather as instructive insight regarding creativity and innovation, which must be understood within ecosocial environments. Because her class focused on introducing students to disciplinary research and writing, Professor Hanson would of course want the students to become familiar with conventional norms in writing. As well, if we ascribe to Sawyer's (2012) argument that creative products or ideas generally work within genre conventions, departing in some ways but not all, we can see that—for this professor and in this classroom—written structure and style were important conventions to adhere to and may even support innovative ways of thinking and doing science.

Perceiving and Judging Creativity and Innovation in Student Work

One key component to understanding creativity and innovation is the judgments put forth by readers regarding a work's departures from convention. In the context of a classroom, such judgments are central and often form the basis of classroom assessment. This Research Methods course was no exception, as the students' research proposals made up 50 percent of the final grade. While feedback was provided to students on components of this proposal throughout the semester, I focused on Professor Hanson's summative assessment of the projects, sitting down with her shortly after the final versions had been read and graded. In this interview, she shared her thoughts on the strong and weak proposals from class, and in doing so also commented on the role of creativity in the students' work. Her emphasis on creativity is interesting because she mentioned it in our interviews prior to my own questions about it; as well, I did not share with her my explicit interest in this element of writing when asking for her consent to participate in the research. Rather, it appeared to be an aspect of research and research genres that held some importance to her.

In our discussion, she consistently pointed to four proposals as being particularly strong, and she noted links between their overall strengths and their creativity: "I see some creativity, some further-along creativity in some of these [proposals]," she commented, "and I think all of the [proposals] that I pointed out as being better are probably better because of that [creativity]" (Interview #2). Here, I offer a closer analysis of three of these four proposals, selected because of Hanson's more detailed comments on these texts, and I follow up with a discussion of one proposal that she identified as particularly weak.

Brooke's Proposal: "Original Thinking"

One student in class, Brooke, had been working with Professor Hanson as a research assistant for nearly two years at the time of my study. Because of their collaboration, Professor Hanson was very familiar with Brooke's work, and indeed this familiarity may have influenced her judgments of creativity in Brooke's research proposal. She described Brooke's work as "original thinking," speculating that she may see it that way "because it's a little different than what I would have come up with" (Interview #2). Brooke's project examined biodiversity and an invasive tree species, *Ailanthus altissima*, found extensively in the urban neighborhood surrounding the university campus. Though invasive species are generally thought to impede biodiversity, Brooke's proposal explored the possibility that *Ailanthus* may in fact have a positive effect on the biodiversity of the local area:

> *Ailanthus* can be found in unlikely places such as narrow alleys and abandoned lots and grows rapidly, both vertically and laterally in its roots. *Ailanthus* can reproduce by seeds and root sprouts, which are an effective way of invading surrounding areas (Heisey and Heisey, 2003). **These qualities could allow** *Ailanthus* **to be used in developing areas in Chicago that need more urban biodiversity.** However, *Ailanthus* has been shown to inhibit the growth and germination of other plants (Heisey, 1990). **This ability to inhibit plant growth may be a mechanism used to overtake areas, in which** *Ailanthus* **would have a negative impact on urban biodiversity.** (Brooke's proposal, boldface added)

Professor Hanson noted this unique logic in the proposal, saying, "I really liked how she played with the idea [. . .] that these invasive species might actually *increase* biodiversity. And she presented some evidence in support of both sides [. . .] so it's interesting either way" (Interview #2).

Brooke's openness to multiple outcomes from her research was made explicit in the final paragraph of her proposal, as she wrote:

> I predict that when insects are introduced to an *Ailanthus* plant, the amount of ailanthone will increase and there will be an increase in biological activity in the roots and leaves as a result. If there is an increase in ailanthone and biological activity after exposure to

insects, then this would suggest an antiherbivore response. If there is no increase in ailanthone, or if there is a decrease in ailanthone, then this raises more interesting questions of the true nature of ailanthone. It is possible that ailanthone may be both an antiherbivore compound and an allelochemical, or that it appears as both because it is an invasive tree species. (Brooke's proposal)

By demonstrating awareness of multiple outcomes, and framing her hypotheses in this way, Brooke appealed to Professor Hanson's suggestion that the students design experiments in which any outcome is interesting.

In describing Brooke's proposal as strong because of its original thinking (including its logical flow and openness to multiple outcomes), Professor Hanson again demonstrated her preference for creative thinking over creative expression—a preference that, as discussed previously, also reflected the ways that she described creativity in class discussions. Indeed, Brooke's proposal seemed to largely conform to expected rhetorical conventions. For instance, her introduction adhered fairly closely to the recommended structure that Professor Hanson had written on the whiteboard in class:

- big idea (why would anybody care?)
- local (specific) question
- your question
- hypothesis at the end of the introduction
- statement of why you expect that outcome.

(Fieldnotes, 28 April 2011)

The only element of this structure that was not present in Brooke's text was a statement of why the outcome was expected; instead, as shown, Brooke articulated an openness to alternative outcomes.

In addition to adopting a relatively conventional rhetorical structure, Brooke's proposal was written in a fairly traditional style. She did use first person and active voice in the final paragraph of her introduction and in her methodology (e.g., *I hope to better understand…, I propose that…, The insects that I will use…, I plan to gather…*), and her proposal included some vivid description that brought the content alive (e.g., Ailanthus *can be found in unlikely places such as narrow alleys and abandoned lots*). However, despite these elements of stance, Brooke's writing style adhered to traditional forms, making extensive use of passive voice and technical jargon. In other words, the form of the proposal—the written expression—was largely conventional, providing additional support for an interpretation of Professor Hanson's judgments of creativity to be grounded in the scientific thinking rather than written expression.

Eileen's Proposal: "A Completely Novel Question"

A second student proposal that Professor Hanson discussed with me in terms of creativity was written by Eileen, whose research examined wetland protection and restoration. Once again, Eileen's proposal stood out to the professor because of its originality. The proposal began by describing wetlands and their importance, including their role in water purification and nutrient recycling and in providing habitats for diverse organisms. Next, the proposal discussed a local wetlands site and the importance of restoration of this site and others. Following this, the proposal made a crucial move, arguing that macroinvertebrates "are potentially very useful for the assessment of wetland restoration success" and noting that:

> Macroinvertebrates have not been widely surveyed at Prairie Wolf Slough, so a more in depth survey of the density, diversity, and assemblage of macroinvertebrates at this site is vital to begin to understand their ecosystem function at the site, and to explore the possibility of using aquatic macroinvertebrates to measure restoration success. (Eileen's proposal)

It was this particular move—applying the question of macroinvertebrates' use in wetland restoration specifically to the local field site—that Professor Hanson found to be so innovative. She explained:

> What makes [Eileen's project] original is that nobody else is doing it. She's got a, a *completely* novel question in a research site that's been extensively studied, and [. . .] she's taking another class right

now, or last quarter, which I think also came to bear on her, on her study. And I like that, I mean I like that she pulled it in and came up with something original. [. . .] bringing in the notion of looking at macroinvertibrates to determine how far along, wetland restoration is, that's—I think that's unique in the Chicagoland area. And I don't know that she realizes just how innovative that is. I don't know how useful it will end up being, but I think it's got huge potential. [. . .] for her to bring that in, I think, show's a lot of creativity on her part. That we could use this site for something that nobody had thought about using the site for. (Interview #2)

As in her evaluation of Brooke's proposal, Professor Hanson showed that she placed high value on novel designs and questions—that is, on creative thinking. It is also interesting to note that Professor Hanson questions whether the innovation here is purposeful when she comments that "I don't know that she realizes just how innovative that is," but the issue of intentionality does not seems to influence the overall judgment that the work is innovative.

Like Brooke's proposal, Eileen's largely followed the organizational structure that Professor Hanson had recommended in class. In fact, in an interview with me, Eileen made note of this broad-to-narrow structure and explained that she had tried to follow it after seeing it in papers and getting feedback and advice from Professor Hanson. Eileen also noted her own preference for adhering to formal conventions rather than trying to depart from them, saying, "I like writing scientific papers because I don't feel like I have to put as much of my own, like, creative input into it. I just, like, report on what it is. Which makes it easier, and I like that" (Eileen's interview).

Frank's Proposal: "Interesting No Matter What the Outcome"

As previously discussed, one of the early course readings, "Strong Inference" (Platt, 1964), encouraged students to design experiments with multiple hypotheses, an approach that Professor Hanson emphasized throughout the Research Methods course. The reading suggested researchers use a logic tree, a visual diagram for exploring the different outcomes that might be followed from the study's data. Although logic trees were discussed in class, visual examples were not provided in the "Strong Inference" reading or in any of the other course readings. Professor Hanson was therefore particularly pleased with Frank's incorporation of a logic tree figure into his final proposal, noting "I was really proud of him" and "I was *so* impressed that he remembered from the beginning of the class that logic tree, [and] then he pulled it into the proposal" (Interview #2).

Professor Hanson's enthusiasm for the proposal wasn't simply due to the fact that Frank had incorporated a logic tree diagram into his proposal but that he had designed a study that would "be interesting no matter what the outcome was" (Interview #2). Unlike the other course proposals, Frank's was very direct about his use of multiple hypotheses, ending his introduction section in the following way:

> I hypothesize that the leafy greens grown at Eden Place have safe lead concentrations as well as better taste and nutritional value than the conventionally grown leafy greens that are available. If I find my results do not support this hypothesis I am determined to understand why, and propose solutions to the problem. (Frank's proposal)

On the one hand, this rhetorical move adhered closely to Hanson's suggestion to include a hypothesis at the end of the introduction (Fieldnotes, 28 April 2012), but at the same time, Frank moved away from the more predictable approach here by also offering the possibility of other outcomes and overtly discussing his own investment in and passion for the issue. In Hanson's words, he "put [himself] in" (Classroom transcript, 5 May 2011) the writing, a strategy that she had encouraged students to take, while not necessarily seeing this as a sign of creativity.

In discussing Frank's proposal with me, Professor Hanson also drew attention to its ability to get "at the heart of the problem"

(Interview #2). Frank's introduction was a bit unique in this regard, as his opening paragraph immediately outlined a very local issue:

> On the south side of Chicago, unused plots of land are being transformed into small-scale urban farms. These urban farms are designed to supply community members with healthy, locally grown, organic produce. In some cases, urban farms are developed on land that was abandoned for environmental health-related reasons. It has been observed that communities do not always respond to the availability of fresh produce the way one would expect. Despite the transformation of these urban sites into land suitable for growing food, some residents are hesitant to purchase this food because they fear it is unsafe due to the previous contamination of the land on which food is grown. There is also an ongoing debate of the benefits of eating organic produce; is it actually more nutritious and better tasting than conventionally grown produce? (Frank's proposal)

It is possible that Frank's direct approach to foregrounding the local concern aids readers in identifying the research problem and influenced Hanson's perception that the proposal got right to the "heart" of the issue.

Professor Hanson further explained to me that, while some students had experience with the systems they were examining in their research, Frank had no specific background with this setting or issue, but "he could just think it out" (Interview #2). My interview with Frank suggested that he worked to think through the system and the multiple hypotheses from the very beginning of the project's design. He referred to the "Strong Inference" reading, stating that:

> . . . you need to be able to ask the next question, already, you know. Before you even do the experiment, think about the experiments you're gonna do with your results [. . .] however they come out. So I guess that's what I was doing, just trying to think through my experiment from the beginning, to some end, with the end being, you know, either these vegetables are safe to be sold at the farmers' market, or they're not. And if they're not, you know, why aren't they? (Frank's interview)

Frank's investment in the issue was also very evident as he spoke in our interview. At one point, he explained bluntly, "You know, these people are basically poisoning themselves, and we have an opportunity to help them, and they need our help" (Frank's interview). This passion for his research was also hinted at throughout Frank's proposal in sentences like, "It is crucial these children are not exposed to any more invisible lead in the food they eat" and "It is uncomfortable to consider that the food one buys at a local farmstand could potentially be poisonous to their customers" (Frank's proposal). This language serves not only to demonstrate the author's stance and attitude toward the research (Hyland, 2008) but also to insert the author into the writing, a technique that, again, Professor Hanson had encouraged. Frank seemed to have strived for this kind of authorial presence in his proposal, saying, "I guess it was just my own research project, and my own proposal, so I felt like I—you know, I wanted to bring my own voice into it. [. . .] I tried to make it readable, but you know, make—kind of bring myself out in it" (Frank's interview). When discussing Frank's proposal with me, Professor Hanson did not note the writing style or strong authorial presence, so it is unclear whether this style influenced her judgment of it as one of the strongest and most creative in class.

Looking more closely at these proposals identified as strong (and creative) by Professor Hanson suggests that her judgments of creativity in this genre were heavily guided by her own understanding of scientific creativity being primarily an issue of creative thought rather than creative expression. While Frank's proposal does demonstrate, in my interpretation, the use of a structure and style that departs at least somewhat from convention, Professor Hanson's comments about it centered entirely on the originality of Frank's thinking about the research. In discussing expectations for proposal structure, Professor Hanson revealed a preference for a "logical" organization that flows smoothly throughout the proposal, and she made note of this attribute in the proposals that she evaluated highly. Although she encouraged students to insert themselves into their scientific writing—and it seems to me that some of these writers strove to do so—she did not make reference to the writers' style or authorial presence in discussing the strengths and weaknesses of their proposals.

Kurt's Proposal: "A Hard Time Telling the Story"

An interesting contrast to Professor Hanson's positive reaction to Brooke's, Eileen's, and Frank's proposals is found in her discussion of Kurt's proposal. As an observer in the class, Kurt stood out to me as a smart and active student, always contributing to classroom discussions and willing to challenge prevailing ideas, as evidenced in the excerpt shared earlier in which he debated the appropriateness of stylistic variation with Professor Hanson. I was somewhat surprised, then, when Professor Hanson identified Kurt's proposal, which focused on the analysis of shark fossils found in the midwestern United States, as one of the two weakest in the class. She explained to me:

> . . . Kurt's [proposal] was weak. He had a hard time wrapping his mind around the project. [. . .] He knew he wanted to work with fossils, but he had no idea what he wanted to do and he couldn't tell a story [in the introduction]. And even at the end he had a hard time telling the story. I think he finally was able to get it, he just . . . he . . . I think a lot of it is that telling the story. (Interview #2)

When I asked her to talk about why she thought he had such difficulty, she explained that the literature in his area was difficult to read but also that Kurt didn't seem to have a sense of purpose or investment in the research:

> . . . what appealed to him was what he would be doing in, in dissolving the bones, or the teeth, and sorting them or comparing them, but he didn't really know why he was doing that. So, he was entering the project more as a research assistant, but we were pushing him to have ownership over a problem. And it took him *quite* a while to get to that point, but he ended up doing a nice proposal. But it—I think it required a lot of time with his advisor, whereas I was able to help all of the other students get closer. (Interview #2)

Professor Hanson's characterization of Kurt's work is interesting when compared with the text of his final proposal. The introduction section, for example, follows fairly closely the proposed general-to-specific structure that Hanson recommended, and it made use of conventional discourse markers such as *In my project, I re-examine...* and *I hypothesize that...*. But the proposal lacks a sense of engagement from the author and primarily describes previous research rather than building an exigence regarding a research problem. Without a clear exigence, it is likely more challenging for the proposal to make a case for a novel contribution. Relevant as well is Professor Hanson's sense that Kurt lacked a strong grasp of the research itself and of why he was doing it, an issue I expand on in the next section.

Possibilities for Creativity and Innovation in the Science Research Classroom

Professor Hanson's assessments of the proposals by Brooke, Eileen, Frank, and Kurt begin to demonstrate the highly contextualized and social nature of receptions of innovation. Here, I dig a bit deeper into the ecosocial environment in which these student genres were produced and evaluated, exploring some of the constraints to and opportunities for creativity and innovation. As Csikszentmihalyi (1999) notes, "Creativity is a process that can be observed only at the intersection where individuals, domains, and fields interact" (p. 314). The ecological systems-based heuristic introduced in Chapter 3 allows one means for examining some of these interactions as they influence the production of innovative or creative instances of a genre.

Viewing the Research Methods classroom as an ecosocial system as Lemke (1993, 1995, 2000) describes it, we might explore "what's going on, what's participating and how, and how one going-on is interdependent with another" (Lemke, 2000, p. 275). At one level, this system includes the domain, where existing norms lie and are made available (to varying degrees) to individuals (Csikszentmihalyi, 1999). The Research Methods setting was influenced by the prevailing norms and conventions of the hard sciences in general and of environmental science[1] more specifically, as well as, more locally, by the environmental

---

[1] Professor Hanson rarely drew distinctions between science in general and environmental science in particular.

science program and the professors and students in it. Within these nested domains, students were exposed to conventional values and practices ranging from preferred forms and uses of language to preferred approaches to knowledge construction. Through the Research Methods course and their other courses, the students became familiar with the dominant disciplinary values of novelty, logic, original thinking, and contribution, and they were required to put these values into practice through a common disciplinary genre. Through course readings and discussions, and through explicit feedback and guidance from Professor Hanson, they began to gain a sense of which disciplinary practices were considered acceptable or even exceptional.

Course readings and discussions offered students glimpses at disciplinary norms not only for doing research but also for presenting that research in written form. All of the research articles that students read were fairly traditional,[2] though Professor Hanson did make note of a few unusual or unconventional features that appeared. Discussions drew students' attention to the value of neutrality and objectivity in science writing and to the riskiness of using "flowery language" or other writing choices that might be unusual. Some students also understood scientific writing as solely fact-based. Ingrid, for example, noted that "you just have facts and you state it" (Ingrid's interview), while Cathy noted the interaction between scientific thinking and expression, stating that "the way I think about things as a scientist [. . .] it would influence the way I write about things. [. . .] I'm more trying to explain things than I am trying to give my interpretation" (Cathy's interview).

It is also important to remember that students were building an understanding of conventions within a classroom environment, a context in which the goal is generally to demonstrate one's ability to adopt dominant norms. In other words, the most immediate domain for the students was one constructed around learning and demonstrating one's learning. They completed their research proposal with the knowledge that it would be read by their advisor and graded by their instructor. Those individuals were positioned as disciplinary experts

---

[2] Notably, many of the non–research oriented articles read in the class, such as the Sand-Jensen (2007) essay, were very non-traditional.

(what Csikszentmihalyi [1999] refers to as field), and their values—including the importance of innovation and creativity in scientific research—very likely influenced the students' choices in the extent to which they wanted to work within convention and in the possibilities they saw for innovative departures. The professor's valuing of creative thought over creative form also mirrors findings in Thaiss and Zawacki's (2006) and Allison's (2004) research, suggesting that such values may be as related to classroom structures as to larger disciplinary spaces. Looking broadly at the system in which these students were participating, then, we see influences of "science," a broadly constructed domain, of their particular field of environmental science, and of the program and classroom in which they were immediately situated. In the next sections, I discuss some of the additional elements of this system that influenced the processes of innovation production and reception within the Research Methods course.

Roles and Hierarchies

Within Research Methods, specific roles were available to individuals, and these roles both afforded and limited their options for innovation. As already mentioned, Professor Hanson held a position of authority in this setting, so her attitudes toward conventions and conformity were important in understanding the possibilities for student innovation. In many ways, Professor Hanson demonstrated an openness to alternative forms and styles. For instance, she assigned the Sand-Jensen (2007) article sarcastically titled "How to Write Consistently Boring Scientific Literature," encouraged students to put themselves into their writing, gave them "permission" to use first-person pronouns and active voice verbs, and didn't require students to change their writing styles even when they were quite informal. Students noted this openness too, with Frank, for instance, stating that "we had a lot of freedom to kind of write whatever we wanted, without any fear of, you know, getting a bad grade" (Frank's interview). In the end, however, Professor Hanson did not make note of students' use of alternative of creative written expression, in positive or negative terms, even explaining to me, "I tend not to notice things like that that, and they don't bother me" (Interview #2). In contrast, she consistently emphasized both an adherence to principles of the scientific method and a drive to look openly and creatively at research problems and data. By rewarding students in classroom discussions with comments like "That's creative!" or "You're thinking like a scientist!" she communicated to students the disciplinary value of such creative thinking as well as her own personal support of it and how creative thinking would be received within the course.

The students, too, played roles within the classroom environment—as learners, novices, research assistants, researchers, and writers. These roles shifted even within a class session, and the shifts were particularly visible on the days that students led discussions of the articles from their own research as they invoked their own experience, knowledge, and goals. In their interviews with me, students also demonstrated their multiple roles and identities and the tensions they felt as researchers responsible for projects they had designed but also as newcomers and novices who lacked the expertise and backgrounds of their mentors. These multiple roles seemed to be a part of Professor Hanson's judgments of the students' work as well, visible in her comments about their knowledge of, engagement in, and ownership over their projects. In describing the two weakest proposals, for instance, Professor Hanson referred to Jaclyn as "not using her mind enough; she's a smart girl, but she's going through the motions and she's not doing the thinking" and to Kurt as "entering the project more as a research assistant, but we were pushing him to have ownership over a problem" (Interview #2). Viewing these individuals as struggling to take on the role of researcher, it seems less likely that Hanson would find any norm-departures in their work to be innovative or creative. Even when she conceded that Kurt had made good revisions to his proposal and "he ended up doing a nice proposal," her impressions of his struggles with the work seemed to influence her overall (perhaps paradoxical) characterization of the proposal as one of the weakest in class. In contrast, Frank, Eileen, and Brooke brought more confidence to their research and demonstrated, to her, more sophistication in the ways in which they drew on established research practices. This demonstration of disciplinary norms built them some symbolic capital and perhaps helped to grant them the role of a "legitimate authority" (Bourdieu, 1991) whose work could be considered creative.

There was, for example, some relationship between those research proposals that Professor Hanson considered to be creative in their thinking and to students' prior research experience and their investment in and ownership over their projects. This proposal was, for most, their first independent research, so they understandably felt like novices and likewise lacked prior experience to draw on in designing their studies and thinking through prior literature. The relative lack of experience may encourage conformity to expectations and caution against creativity or originality. Professor Hanson speculated that, for some students, "experience with the systems [they were studying] made them be more creative and better able to tell the story" (Interview #2), but she also acknowledged that one of the most creative projects was by a student (Frank) who had no prior experience with the system or with independent research. Whether or not they had had previous research experience, some students took strong ownership over their projects while others saw themselves as largely supporting a faculty member's research. Contrast, for example, Frank's and Cathy's comments:

> This will definitely be the first research project where I feel like I'm kind of more on my own. Last summer I did a little bit—like an introduction to research project but there was seven or eight people working on the project. So I'm pretty excited to kind of get to do it myself. Because I feel like I like working with people but I also like working by myself. (Frank's interview)

> . . . it was more the conversations with Dr. Taylor [that influenced me], because this is, well her—pretty much her—not her project because she's, you know—this just a small part of what she's trying to do [. . .]. But, you know she just like really knows the literature, and stuff like that, because she's been working on it for so long. So she was really influential. (Cathy's interview)

For some students, then, it seems as though prior experience and a sense of ownership gave them the kind of confidence in their projects that might foster a willingness to take risks and think outside the box.

These same factors also appear linked to students' approaches to more creative expression within their texts. The proposal genre was new to all of the Research Methods students, and several commented in interviews that they were at times confused by what the text itself should look like, since they did not read sample proposals in class. Given their lack of familiarity with the text-genre, they faced some challenges in employing conventions, a seeming prerequisite for *bending* those conventions in ways that experts will find appropriate (Sawyer, 2012).

Yet not all students who were invested in and passionate about their projects desired to play with generic form in their writing. In fact, four of the five students I interviewed explained that they sought to conform to convention rather than breaking from it, citing reasons such as not wanting to be too risky (Hannah), trying to conform to the teacher's expectations (Cathy), liking traditional scientific writing (Ingrid), and liking "writing scientific papers because I don't feel like I have to put as much of my own creative input into it" (Eileen). In these cases, it is not surprising that students sought to learn the traditional conventions and work within them before attempting to play with them. Notably, the individuals I followed in Research Methods were novices positioned in the roles of learners, clearly subordinate in experience and power to their instructor and advisors who would evaluate their work. Awareness of this positioning was quite likely to also influence many of these writers and their approaches to creativity and innovation.

Access, Availability, and Collaboration

Because scientific research is highly collaborative, access to resources—including social networks—can be pivotal to one's participation. While all of the students in Research Methods worked with an advisor, the relationships and nature of the collaboration varied considerably. Those students who were more involved in research teams or who had worked as a research assistant were given more access to the kinds of practices preferred by experts. Notably, the two proposals that Professor Hanson identified as the weakest in class were written by students who were not participating in research teams or collaborating closely with their faculty advisors. The kind of access afforded by such collaborations might have bolstered their engagement in research and, thus, their familiarity with preferred practices. With more limited access to disciplinary practices, these students would also seem to have more limited opportunities for learning to appropriate and play with genres in ways considered effective by experts. Perhaps more important is the role that collaborative dialogue itself seems to play in the generation of novel ideas and insights in scientific inquiry (Sawyer, 2012). Without such networked participation, learners cannot benefit from the give-and-take that often leads to scientific creativity.

Although the classroom aimed to introduce students to disciplinary research practices, it was necessarily constrained by the typical features of a classroom, providing only attenuated access to the genres and other resources that characterize disciplinary practice. It did provide access to one important genre (the research article), and several students noted the value of this exposure in their interviews, sharing that they now felt much more comfortable reading disciplinary research. At the same time, the course did not expose students directly to the forms or practices of the proposal genre that they were asked to produce, and several students shared with me the challenge they felt in preparing a proposal without ever having seen one. Frank, for example, explained:

> I did feel like at the beginning of the course, I didn't really know what we were getting ourselves into, and even halfway through, I was still kind of confused, like what is this? Is this a *real* proposal, is this just, you know, something I'm working on for this class? [...] also, you know, we were reading all these research papers that had introductions and methods, and I was like, am I supposed to write this thing like I've already done the experiment, or is this actual—an actual proposal. (Frank's interview)

On the one hand, the lack of exposure to examples of the genre (both in form but also in research practices) may have fostered less conventional writing or research practices, but it may also have constrained opportunities for intentional innovation, as students felt they lacked a strong understanding of conventions and of the kinds of variations and innovation that were possible and rewarded.

Novelty, Originality, and Genre

The value placed on novelty and originality has already been mentioned in much of my discussion. Within the Research Methods course, the larger disciplinary values of novelty, originality, and contribution were frequently referred to. In one class discussion, for example, Professor Hanson reminded students that work is considered publishable when it is novel and offers a contribution (Fieldnotes, 14 April 2011). My own perception was that Professor Hanson's message was fairly unambiguous—novelty and originality were important in research design and data analysis. It was this kind of novelty that was praised as students discussed research articles and offered ideas for follow-up research. Generic forms, on the other hand, were presented as a riskier place for originality. While Professor Hanson did acknowledge changes in lexico-grammatical conventions over time and differences in individual preferences for these, larger rhetorical structures for organizing information were presented in more static ways. Personal style, in other words, was downplayed though not explicitly discouraged.

At the heart of this layered social system of research learning is the genre of focus: a student research proposal. The writer's role of "student" is important here because it distinguishes the genre from proposals written by disciplinary experts, typically produced to request project funding from an institution or organization. A student research proposal, in contrast, is written for teachers or advisors who will grant permission to move forward with the project. As a classroom research genre, the proposal also holds the aim of demonstrating to a gatekeeper (such as an instructor, advisor, or committee) the student's knowledge of the discipline's content and conventions; student proposals may ultimately receive a grade or mark, further distinguishing them from professional research proposals. The practices for carrying out this classroom genre are carefully guided and scaffolded by an instructor, with support through formative feedback along the way. Opportunities for innovative thinking had to be largely carried out within this structured practice. Furthermore, the forms of classroom research genres like this one are usually locally defined and constrained. In the case of Research Methods, handouts and class discussions framed the possibilities for response or uptake and heavily steered students toward the creation of a proposal that followed a fairly prescribed form: an introduction (which mimicked the structure of a research article introduction), followed by short methods section, a brief timeline, and finally a bibliography.

As Russell (1997) has demonstrated, classroom genres are intertextually linked to other disciplinary genres, which are themselves embedded in disciplinary ideologies and values. Therefore, in science classrooms, it is typical to see genres guided by the discursive practices of hard-knowledge disciplines, including beliefs in empiricism with scientists "act[ing] as if they see themselves as discovering truth, not making it" (Hyland, 2000, p. 33). These values and practices were emphasized to the Research Methods students through course readings, classroom discussions, faculty guest talks, and the scaffolding of the proposal assignment.

The hard sciences are notable as well in their use of very conventionalized forms for sharing new knowledge (Bazerman, 1988). Even highly original work tends to conform to established generic practices, with researchers closely relating their work to prior knowledge and research. Professor Hanson often stressed formal genre conventions in class, such as a preferred structure for introductions, and she encouraged students to look to the research articles they read as models. In an interview with me, she described scientific writing as fairly formulaic, and in class she taught a template-like introduction format to students. Similarly, when discussing publishing in academic journals, Professor Hanson reminded students that journals offer instructions on organizing articles, and that "you must meet the journal's requirements" (Fieldnotes, 14 April 2011). Through such discussions, students likely came to understand the proposal genre—and science research genres more generally—as welcoming novelty and contribution in the content and design of their work but discouraging radical departures from conventionalized text forms. To borrow Bhatia's (2006) terms, the student research proposal, as carried out in this particular context, might be categorized as a relatively conservative genre in form and practice.

Production and Reception of Innovation as a Situated Process

This chapter has offered a fairly detailed view of how one classroom setting constructed innovation and creativity in disciplinary research genres, and how possibilities for such innovation were both facilitated and constrained by the ecosocial context. This research suggests that creativity and innovation are possible and may even be rewarded within classroom contexts but that that their production and reception are shaped by multiple layers of the social environment. Importantly, the study also demonstrates some of the ways in which possibilities for student innovation may differ from the possibilities available to those in more experienced roles.

Reception of norm-departures within a classroom environment is influenced by the nested layers of disciplinary, institutional, local, and individual practice. Within Research Methods, for example, creative approaches to generic form were not highly valued, and these values were influenced by the course goals, the professor's preferences, the environmental science department faculty, and the disciplinary field— which is not to say that all of these social groups and their individuals discouraged innovative forms of research genres. Rather, the dominant message that students received was that innovative forms might be risky or simply unnecessary. Similar courses in other disciplines, however, would likely offer different possibilities for innovation, with some perhaps encouraging language play or even hybridized or alternative generic forms. Disciplines that place a high value on critique of dominant discourses and social structures, for instance, may be more likely to expose students to highly variable generic forms and to encourage students to challenge or critique traditional conventions. Becher and Trowler (2001) similarly note that "soft" disciplines with weaker boundaries may be more open to innovation. Possibilities for innovation, then, are deeply embedded in disciplinary ideologies, histories, and social structures, but simultaneously situated within very local settings and relations.

What I hope I have demonstrated through the research in this chapter is the need for a highly ecological understanding of genre innovation. To simply acknowledge that genres are variable and that experts, eventually, develop an ability to appropriate or manipulate them is to skim over the fascinating nuances of innovation. Innovation is as complex, as situated, and as deeply embedded in ecosocial systems as convention—though it has been much less explored. What seems particularly salient is the need to view genre innovation as much more than breaks from traditional forms but instead to understand innovation potential as residing in genres' forms, content, practices, ideologies, and epistemologies and taking place within layered and complex social environments. With this need in mind, I now turn to the question of how such a view of genre innovation might be relevant to the teaching of academic writing.

Chapter 5

Genre Innovation in the
Academic Writing Classroom

In genre studies, the classroom has always been one of the biggest sites of contention amongst scholars and teachers, with concerns about the extent to which genres can and should be taught given their dynamic and situated nature. The danger, as articulated most boldly perhaps by Freedman (1993), is that, when brought into the classroom, genres will be presented and presumably learned as static formulas or templates, de-coupled from the rhetorical contexts and communities that give them meaning. A static, "a-rhetorical" view of text, of course, contradicts much of what scholars now understand about academic writing. As demonstrated by a great deal of work in the past few decades—much of it reviewed in Chapters 2 and 3 of this book—we know academic genres to be in constant flux and characterized by variation, and we know that individual writers often take liberties with their texts as they adapt genres for their own purposes and motivations. Indeed, discussions have repeatedly described the exploitation and manipulation of genres as the behavior of expert users and as a goal of genre instruction (e.g., Bawarshi, 2003; Bhatia, 2004; Devitt, 2004; Hyland, 2007). A second and equally important concern regarding genre-based instruction is that it can serve to reproduce existing genre norms thereby reifying rather than challenging dominant structures of power (e.g., Benesch, 2001; Luke, 1996). One counter to these claims has been that genres are changed from within and that therefore making the normalized forms and practices visible to learners better positions them—indeed, may be *necessary*—for genre appropriation and change.

Though these issues are often framed as either/or propositions (one teaches genres or does not), excluding genres from the classroom is not really an option, as they are a primary means through which humans communicate in writing. The question is not whether genres should be taught but rather how instruction can best facilitate learners' ability to use genres effectively. To be fair, as Hyland (2007) and others have pointed out, genre-based instruction certainly can fall into the trap that critics fear, particularly if teachers themselves hold more static views of genre or if local policies and curricular goals constrain possibilities for classroom practices. But much of what has been written about genre-based pedagogy encourages learners to explore the variation, and by extension perhaps the innovation, inherent to genre. Therefore, many of the ideas that I share in this chapter are not new to genre-based teaching. What I hope to contribute is a more extended discussion of the role that genre innovation may hold in the academic writing classroom, along with several example activities and assignments.

I need to state upfront, though, that the primary aim of this chapter is not to argue for a teaching approach that focuses on flouting conventions and challenging generic norms. Such an approach may be as limiting—if not more so—than one that teaches formulaic versions of texts. Instead, innovation must be contextualized within a broader approach to genre that explores conventions and norms in depth. The assumption that underlies this chapter, then, is that part of building knowledge of specific genres and rhetorical awareness of how genres work more generally involves developing an understanding of the innovation potential in genres—that is, the creativity and variation that writers themselves bring to any generic activity and the socio-rhetorical dimensions that influence the reception of such innovation. With a focus on enriching learners' genre knowledge and awareness, the practices I discuss here can also, in part, address concerns that classroom teaching will default to a genre-as-template orientation and that genre-based pedagogy serves the interests of dominant users at the expense of the diverse and often marginalized voices of learners.

In this chapter, then, I wade into the sometimes murky waters of genre and pedagogy. I begin by reviewing some of the key points made about genre innovation so far in this book, hoping to highlight issues of relevance for genre learning and teaching. Next, I outline some theoretical and empirical support for the inclusion of genre innovation in writing instruction. The latter half of this chapter then offers some principles and practices for incorporating innovation as a means of building genre knowledge and genre awareness.

Key Features of Genre Innovation

In the previous chapters, I have attempted to tease apart some features of innovation that are of value for our understanding of genre theory and genre learning. Here, I review these again with a particular eye toward classroom support.

One key issue involves the kinds of unconventionalities that might fall under a conception of "genre innovation." Innovative forms often attract the most attention for readers because they are so visible. But if we understand genre to be a social category—a process rather than a product, as Prior (2009) argues—we need to think beyond form when considering opportunities for innovation. To review, some potential frameworks for understanding kinds of genre innovation relate to discourse disruption (language, text, and world schemata) (Cook, 1994), alternative approaches (formats, ways of conceptualizing and arranging arguments, syntaxes, methodologies, and media) (Thaiss & Zawacki, 2006), and genre knowledge dimensions (form, rhetoric, content, and practices) (Tardy, 2009). A synthesis of these frameworks is offered in Figure 5.1, which broadly considers genre innovation as occurring in linguistic and textual form, modality, rhetorical aims and strategies, content, and practice or processes. These categories certainly are not discrete (can we, for example, distinguish between innovative content and practice in the case of an unusual research design?), but they offer at least a general approach to imagining innovation beyond form. The various levels, as well, help to account for assessments of a text being innovative even when it reflects a prototypical form, as in the case of parodies or texts that subtly remix or mock related texts.

Figure 5.1. Areas of Genre Innovation in Academic Writing

Area of Genre Innovation	Examples from Academic Writing
Linguistic and textual form	Unusual word choices; non-canonical grammar forms; mixing of linguistic codes; unconventional move structures
Modality	Integration of unconventional modalities; use of an uncommon modality for that genre
Rhetorical aims and strategies	Unconventional use of stance or engagement markers; use of rhetorical appeals uncommon to the genre
Content	Incorporation of unusual or unexpected ideas
Practice	Unique approaches to research methodology, design, or composing processes

Because genres carry out social actions, it is also useful to keep in mind that innovations, when intentional, are motivated by authors' aims within the genre. As reviewed in Chapter 3, these aims may be numerous and include reaching alternative ways of understanding an issue or constructing knowledge; expressing oneself in unique ways; engaging readers; and resisting, changing, and critiquing dominant discourses. Such goals may be realized through various approaches to innovation as appropriate and effective within a particular situation.

This last point is critical and is something I've emphasized throughout this book, and that is that innovation is not an inherent quality but rather is a value assigned by others. Such judgment or reception occurs within a complex ecological and social environment, so that some kinds of innovation may be more or less welcome in a particular setting. For instance, the undergraduate instructors in studies by Thaiss and Zawacki (2006) and Allison (2004), as well as my own study in Chapter 4, suggest that innovative content may be more welcomed in classroom environments than innovative form. The point here, though, is not to generalize but rather to consider the reception of unconventional texts within their complex ecosocial environments. The writers, readers, genres, stakes and outcomes, policies, and institutional and disciplinary values are just some of the many components of this complex and interactive system that shape such receptions. The issue of reception is central to understanding genre innovation (and, indeed, genre) more generally but is of particular value when considering the teaching and learning of genres within classroom settings. As students learn to negotiate the expectations for academic literacy in a range of classrooms and other academic activities, they can be supported by attending to reception. Put another way, a role of the classroom might be to help writers understand the "rhetorical options available to them and *the effects* of manipulating these options for interactional purposes" (Hyland, 2012, p. 146, emphasis added).

A Theoretical Rationale for Innovation in the Writing Classroom

On initial reflection, innovation may seem to be a concept that is irrelevant to writing instruction, at least for most learners. Because we often associate innovation with experts, we might think of it as a part of writing better delayed for very advanced courses or perhaps simply for writers who are beyond the realm of formal writing instruction. I want to suggest, though, that there is a place for innovation even in classrooms for novice writers. In this section I address some theoretical rationale for such integration before proceeding to describe some more specific classroom practices.

Language Play in Second Language Learning

One small but growing area of research that has much potential to contribute to our understanding of genre innovation and writing instruction is the study of language play (LP) in second language learning. This scholarship has tended to distinguish between *rehearsal language play*, which is likened to the Vygotskyan notion of inner speech/private speech (Lantolf, 1997), and *ludic language play*, which aligns with Cook's (2000) exploration (described in Chapter 2) of the playful and often humorous disruptions to language norms. Ludic LP is the most immediately relevant to a discussion of genre play and innovation.

Adopting a ludic orientation to LP, Tarone (2002) has defined language play as "the expression of the speaker's creativity in deliberately, consciously choosing to violate normal expectancies of language use by playing off different varieties against one another, for the sheer purpose of enjoyment and entertainment" (p. 293). Though more restricted than the broader notion of genre innovation explored in this book, Tarone's definition of LP similarly draws attention to the multivoicedness or heteroglossia (Bakhtin, 1981) that may underlie purposeful norm departures. Drawing on Cook (2000), Tarone (2002) also notes that advanced language users are likely more agile in their LP, playing with both language forms and also "semantic worlds," as in the case of parody. Studies of ludic LP have looked at formal play through the use of features like phonological repetition, puns, rhyming, humor, and code-mixing. Semantic play has been studied through examples in which activities provide students a separation from "real-world" references, assuming roles and new voices. Classroom LP seems to offer motivating opportunities for departing from a focus on accuracy and for flouting social norms. Perhaps unsurprisingly, then, as in the case of non-classroom LP, research seems to suggest that language play is not at all rare in language classrooms, and for some learners it may be very frequent.

Language play does not seem to be important simply because it is common; rather, several scholars have maintained that LP has a role in second language acquisition. Tarone (2000) considers how two important models for understanding language acknowledge the role of play and creativity: (1) Bakhtin's (1981) view of language use as always encompassing the tensions of normalizing (centripetal) forces and individual creativity and diversity (centrifugal forces) and (2) Larsen-Freeman's (1997) description of language as a complex, dynamic system. Within both models, Tarone argues, there is an important place for language play because it exemplifies the *unpredictability* of individuals' language use. Tarone goes further, though, in considering whether LP can actually support language acquisition. While she acknowledges that LP is not necessary for such acquisition, she and others (Broner & Tarone, 2001; Cekaite & Aronsson, 2005; Tarone, 2000, 2002) have pointed to several ways in which it may facilitate the process:

○ The fun nature of LP may make the L2 discourse more noticeable and thus more memorable (Tarone, 2000, 2002). Cekaite and Aronsson (2005) describe LP as "affectively charged" (p. 170).

○ The use of semantic play (e.g., the creation of fictional worlds or parody) can engage learners in double-voicing as they take on new social roles, thereby supporting development of sociolinguistic competence (Tarone, 2000, 2002).

○ The use of LP brings greater variation into the interlanguage (IL) system, and this increased variation is actually necessary for development of a complex dynamic IL system (Tarone, 2000). In Tarone's (2002) words, the counterbalancing force of creativity and play "may, among other things, help to promote a certain permeability, or openness to change, in the interlanguage, thus preventing fossilization and promoting further development" (p. 294). In other words, an IL system requires instability in order for it to develop; language play, innovation, and creativity introduce such instability. By bringing language play into the classroom, teachers might foster this productive tension between standardized norms and individual creativity that can facilitate learning (Broner & Tarone, 2000).

○ LP can provide opportunities of authentic language use, thereby preparing students for non-classroom conversations (Cekaite & Aronsson, 2005).

○ It may serve a face-saving strategy, giving students freedom to experiment with less common forms (Cekaite & Aronsson, 2005; van Dam, 2002).

○ It can extend collaborative engagement, focus group attention on form, and create more opportunities for language practice (Cekaite & Aronsson, 2005).

Studies of classroom-based second language play have included young learners (Cekaite & Aronsson, 2005; Tarone, 2000) and adults (Belz & Reinhardt, 2004; Bushnell, 2008; Waring, 2013; Warner, 2004) primarily in foreign language classrooms. The majority of this research has focused exclusively on oral language interactions, but a few studies have looked at language play through computer-mediated written communication. Belz and Reinhardt (2004) traced the LP of a university-level German L2 learner through his chat and email messages with German keypals and found numerous examples of word play and the appropriation and re-voicing of words. The learner described his frequent use of LP as a pleasurable activity, one that he engaged in for fun, but the researchers also describe it as functioning to enhance his learning of new aspects of language, to consolidate his existing grammatical knowledge, to build personal relationships, to present a positive face to his keypals, and to index his growing multicompetence.

This work on learners' desire to play with language resonates with academic writing too. I suspect that many readers will be able to think of examples of their own attempts at self-amusement in academic writing—my Facebook newsfeed somewhat regularly includes posts by academic friends amusingly sharing their attempts to incorporate unexpected words or references into their academic papers. It is notable not just that they do so in their writing but also that they desire to share their "covert" practices. A group of Swedish scientists similarly revealed their long-running competition to incorporate lyrics from Bob Dylan's songs into their academic papers (though not in traditional research articles), giving rise to titles such as "The Biological Role of Nitrate and Nitrite: The Times They Are a-Changin'" (Michaels, 2014). This interest that experienced writers have in playing with a discourse that often appears so rigid is noteworthy but also seems somewhat removed from reality for many novice writers, who often experience academic writing as a rule-based system. One fruitful area of research could examine the extent to which playful uses of academic writing are related to experience, a sense of ownership, and expertise.

Though most research into language play has shied away from explicit pedagogical implications (with the exception of a growing body of work on digital games—e.g., Sykes & Reinhardt, 2012)—Broner and Tarone (2000) do make such a case directly. They argue for the value of bringing language play into the classroom primarily because it creates the kind of productive tension between standardized norms and individual creativity that can support learning. Kramsch and Sullivan (1996) have also called for pedagogical approaches that foster language play, particularly in foreign language classrooms, allowing learners to maintain "a playful distance" (p. 211) from dominant conventions. This tensions between norms and creative, playful variation is of course also central to genre and is at the heart of concerns raised by critics who fear that explicit instruction of genres may tilt the balance toward normativity and away from diversity.

Theoretical and empirical explorations of language play offer a useful correlate to the potential for genre play in enhancing learners' developing systems of genre knowledge. At the same time, while the evidence of some value in language (or genre) play seems valid, it is also important not to over-emphasize its role. Because LP involves playing with conventional patterns, it relies (heavily) on knowledge of convention as well.

World Englishes, Alternative Discourses, and Writing Instruction

Tension between conformity and diversity has also been at the center of much scholarship in world Englishes, a field that has closely studied language varieties and the ways in which such varieties evolve through local users and uses. At the heart of the world Englishes (WE) paradigm is the pluricentric view that there is no one, stable English but rather numerous varieties of English, each with their own histories, users, functions, contexts of use, and identities. Many of these varieties have been developed by non-native English speakers. Braj Kachru (1988) modeled these multiple Englishes as geographically situated within Inner Circle countries (where English is a dominant native language), Outer Circle countries (where English has a colonial history and carries out important functions in society, often as an official language), and Expanding Circle countries (where English is a common foreign language).

Much attention in WE scholarship has been on oral communication, at least in part because features of written language (e.g., codified spelling, formal register, and a need to restrict ambiguity) tend to have a stabilizing effect and erase many of the variations that are found in spoken language. But WE variation goes beyond linguistic features to encompass larger pragmatic and rhetorical issues, which are also, of course, important in academic genres. To illustrate this, Yamuna Kachru (1997) has described the distinct practices surrounding Indian wedding invitations. While a wedding invitation in the U.S. or U.K. may arrive through the mail with no previous oral interaction, Kachru explains that social norms in India require a face-to-face invitation prior to the written text. The written invitation also has other unique rhetorical and formal features and these distinct conventions relate to the sociocultural setting and the goals for the genre within that setting.

Implications of WE for the language classroom are significant. Once a multiplicity of norms is assumed, which norms should be taught and assessed? Where and when? Aya Matsuda (2012a) has stated that:

> . . . pedagogy that introduces students only to the English varieties, people and culture of the Inner Circle countries is simply inadequate. In order to prepare effective users of EIL [English as an International Language], some significant changes must occur in both teachers' and learners' mindsets as well as the specific classroom practices." (p. 5)

The kinds of changes that Matsuda and others have outlined reorient the issue from simply one of "which variety should be taught?" to also one of "which concepts are essential for using English effectively in international contexts?" (see Matsuda, 2012b). Matsuda identifies sociopolitical awareness, communication strategies, and linguistic competence as examples of such concepts. Building on these ideas, Kubota (2012) further draws attention to the multilingualism that characterizes the environments in which EIL is used, and she also points to "critical awareness of power and privilege as essential in border-crossing communication" (p. 63). Such a focus, she argues, is necessary for challenging monolingual assumptions and affirming global and local diversity.

Though little attention in general has been given to the teaching of writing within a WE or EIL orientation, Matsuda and Matsuda (2010, pp. 371–373) do address this challenge, identifying five pedagogical principles for helping students negotiate the tensions between dominant norms and diversification:

1. Teach the dominant language forms and functions.
2. Teach the non-dominant language forms and functions.
3. Teach the boundary between what works and what does not.
4. Teach the principles and strategies of discourse negotiation.
5. Teach the risks involved in using deviational features.

Power is an important concept for them as well as they point to the risks often involved in negotiating or challenging dominant norms. As such, they caution teachers against "overly valoriz[ing] either the dominant discourses or alternative discourses" (p. 373), and they simultaneously call on teachers to play a role in challenging the power of such discourses.

Although the broad range of WE scholarship has not garnered significant attention within rhetoric and composition studies, scholars like Canagarajah (2002, 2006a, 2013) and Matsuda (2006, 2013; also Matsuda & Matsuda, 2011) have helped bring attention to the plurality and sociopolitical complexity of English in a multilingual, global environment and the relevance of these issues to U.S. writing instruction. While the notion of world Englishes may be relatively new to many compositionists, it aligns with existing conversations in the field in which scholars have advocated for alternative discourses (Schroeder, Fox, & Bizzell, 2002; Thaiss & Zawacki, 2006) or, dating even further back, "students' right to their own languages" (Perryman-Clark, Kirkland, & Jackson, 2014; Smitherman, 2003). Work in these areas has not tended to focus on the playful enjoyment of experimentation—at least not to the extent of scholarship in language play—but rather on the opportunities for writers to assert their own identities as authors, challenging, resisting, and perhaps ultimately transforming dominant norms.

More recently, these issues in composition studies have become associated with a paradigm of translingualism. In the first published discussion of a translingual approach within composition studies, Horner et al. (2011) described this approach as seeing "language differences and fluidities as resources to be preserved, developed, and utilized" (p. 304). In the classroom, they suggested that such an approach might focus on critical reflection and awareness of language and linguistic heterogeneity. Related discussions have argued for a pedagogy that emphasizes the negotiation of discursive forms, thereby disrupting normative conventions and perhaps even social structures (Canagarajah, 2006a).

One strategy that has been offered as a means of such disruption is codemeshing,[1] defined by Canagarajah (2013) as the bringing together of different semiotic resources in new ways in order to resist dominant norms from within. Canagarajah (2006a, 2013) has repeatedly noted that this strategy places high demands on minority writers:

> It demands proficiency in established varieties, expert use of local variants, and the rhetorical strategies of meshing. In other words, this strategy requires not only awareness of the established and local norms, but the competence to bring them together strategically for voice and for one's objectives. Codemeshing calls for complex linguistic and rhetorical competence. (2013, p. 125)

In many ways, the strategy reflects the process of bilinguals' creativity described in WE scholarship—manipulating texts as a way of mediating established and local norms—and it also responds to Kubota's (2012) call for helping students to develop critical awareness of border-crossing communication. But while codemeshing or other strategies for producing alternative discourses can be used to effectively innovate genres, their integration into the writing classroom should be carried out with caution.

One concern relates to the need for "proficiency in established varieties" that Canagarajah refers to. Many multilingual writers, for

---

[1] This particular use of the term has been critiqued by Matsuda (2013).

example, are still building their proficiency in established varieties, so negotiation of multiple varieties may not yet be a realistic or appropriate goal. Related is the role of convention that is explicitly acknowledged by Canagarajah (2013) and also by Matsuda (2002), who has emphasized the importance of engaging students with dominant discourses and conventions "because alternative discourses are always defined in relation to dominant discourses in a particular context" (pp. 195–196). Convention and established norms, then, may even be more important in such an approach, though their exploration may be pursued with the kind of critical awareness of power and privilege that Kubota (2012) calls for.

Further, several questions arise in relation to the use of alternative discourses by student or novice writers: Who is granted the right to adopt these practices? In what genres and activities? For whom? Within which communities? On what topics? While illustrations of disruptive discourse by notable scholars are instructive, they may also be misleading to novice writers. Indeed, much of what we know about genre manipulation and innovation demonstrates the importance of understanding both conventions and the power-laden ecologies of text production and reception. As I have attempted to demonstrate throughout this book, such an ecological view is essential to genre and therefore should also be a part of instruction. In other words, classroom integration of alternative discourses should actively engage students in exploring texts from this perspective so that they have a realistic view of both the opportunities and constraints available to them.

It is also worth noting that much of the work on alternative discourses has focused on formal and rhetorical text innovations but has not considered the fuller range of opportunities that exist when genre is viewed as social action—this broader emphasis is especially important given the possibility that innovations to content may be valued over innovations to form outside of the writing classroom (Allison, 2004; Thaiss & Zawacki, 2006). As well, there is, as Kopelson (2014) has described, "a tendency to fetishize the different and demonize the dominant" (p. 217) within this scholarship, and most frequently this is found in discussions of text forms. Familiarizing students with various approaches to innovation (as described in Figure 5.1) and the extent to which different genres, communities, and settings shape these options may provide a richer view of alternative discourses and simultaneously work to counter *de facto* assumptions of genres as merely text forms.

Finally, with these caveats in mind, I'd like to draw some connection between these discussions of world Englishes, alternative discourses, and language play. With its focus on fun manipulation, language play may be an attractive complement to or component of a critical, resistance-oriented pedagogy, as it can offer motivations for exploiting dominant norms that are more related to identity or enjoyment and less related to a riskier goal of changing an existing power structure—a goal that not all students may share. Likewise, strategies of hybridity and discourse disruptions can offer valuable means for having fun with language and genre.

Overall, while I am less persuaded of the *universal* appropriateness of a resistance-oriented approach to teaching writing, I find compelling the research in biliteracy that suggests multilingual writers can benefit from opportunities to draw on their own multiple linguistic resources (see, for example, Cummins, 2007, 2009; Gentil, 2011, in press). I also find the emphasis on critical awareness—in discussions of both English as an international language and translingualism—to be of relevance to writing and language development and its related pedagogy. If some students use this awareness to serve their own aims, all the better, but to do this they will need a robust, ecological understanding not just of language but also of genre and discourse.

Genre Knowledge and Genre Awareness

As should be clear, insights from scholarship on language play, world Englishes, and alternative discourses offer potential resources for addressing the concerns related to genre-based pedagogy. They also align well with the notions of genre knowledge and genre awareness, both central to genre-informed instruction, as they relate to users' ability not just to mimic forms but rather to exploit and manipulate them. I will first tease apart these two concepts, expanding on how innovation contributes to each.

In general, scholars have used the term *genre knowledge* to refer to the understanding of specific genres that users hold (Berkenkotter & Huckin, 1995; Bhatia, 1999). For experts, genre knowledge appears to be multidimensional, integrating several knowledge domains such as text form, subject-matter content, practices and processes for carrying out genres, and rhetoric (Tardy, 2009). These four domains are, of course, reductive given the complexities involved. Whether they include or might need to be augmented by other kinds of knowledge, such as metaknowledge (Gentil, 2011) or epistemological knowledge (Kuteeva, 2013), is a worthy question though less immediately important for my purpose here. What is relevant is that the genre knowledge of experts seems to be characterized by very sophisticated (though not necessarily conscious) understanding of many textual, social, and conceptual areas. This knowledge is drawn upon when writers manipulate and exploit genres for their own purposes. Put another way, expert genre knowledge supports an understanding of how to exploit and innovate generic activity. As Bhatia (1997), cautions, however, genre knowledge is itself insufficient for successful innovation to genre because success also hinges on situations of use and the authority of the user (Kress, 1987) and many other elements of the ecosocial system.

In his rich theoretical exploration of biliteracy and genre knowledge, Gentil (2011) explores the relations among writing expertise, language proficiency, and genre knowledge. He also calls attention to the important role of metaknowledge, or "the explicit understanding of specific genres and of genre as a concept" (p. 10). Demonstrating how multilinguals are often able to harness their broad linguistic and discursive resources as they learn and use genres in multiple languages and communities, Gentil posits that metaknowledge may assist in this process. Multilingual genre learning, he argues, potentially has a great deal of value, as it may "promote genre awareness, rhetorical flexibility, and audience sensitivity" (p. 20). Gentil's discussion usefully links genre knowledge and awareness, with awareness playing a potential role in supporting genre knowledge. Negretti and Kuteeva (2011) similarly link these concepts, using the term *metacognitive genre awareness* to describe "metacognitive processes that have as their object knowledge of genre, discourse, and rhetorical aspects of academic texts" (p. 96).

Such processes might be carried out in genre analysis, for example, as students' attention is drawn to various aspects of a genre and their interrelations. Cheng's (2007, 2011) studies of multilingual writers in graduate-level genre-based writing courses suggest that even a focus on a specific feature of one genre may contribute to developing more general genre awareness for learners. It should be noted, however, that the students in Cheng's research were already advanced writers and language users.

Genre awareness is at least in part characterized by explicit or conscious understanding. It is defined by Devitt (2009) as "a conscious attention to genres and their potential influences on people and the ability to consider acting differently within genres" (p. 347). We might understand it to be a general rhetorical understanding of how genres function for people in specific activities and communities. For Johns (2008), genre awareness is important for helping students develop "the rhetorical flexibility necessary for adapting their socio-cognitive genre knowledge to ever-evolving contexts" (p. 239). Because it is not tied to knowledge of a specific genre, genre awareness has become an important focus for scholars concerned with general academic writing contexts, such as first-year undergraduate writing courses, where students' future genre needs are often too diverse or unpredictable to be directly addressed in such courses.

With its emphasis on rhetorical flexibility, it would seem that innovation also has a role to play in genre awareness. An understanding of the variation that is inherent to genre, for example, should also encompass an awareness of the dynamics at play in the reception of variation, including more extreme variations that might ultimately be deemed innovative or unsuccessful. In sum, innovation is relevant to both genre awareness and genre knowledge: Rich genre awareness might include an understanding of the possibilities for genre innovation, while sophisticated genre knowledge might include an understanding of such possibilities within a particular genre.

Returning to the more immediate concerns of writing instruction, the relative importance of genre-specific knowledge will vary by classroom and educational context. The memo-writing courses I taught at a multinational company in Japan, for example, were designed very specifically around the goal of building students' knowledge of the locally idiosyncratic approach to memo-writing within the company, though I hoped that they would develop more general genre awareness through the courses as well. In contrast, when I teach writing to first-year university students for when English is an additional language, helping them to develop genre awareness is more important to me, as it is impossible to predict the specific genres that will feature prominently in their individual academic and professional trajectories. With the broad range of classrooms in which genre-based approaches are now used—including foreign language, elementary and secondary, undergraduate, graduate, and workplace courses—the relative emphasis on genre knowledge and genre awareness is something that each teacher must weigh. As I understand genre-based approaches, the general principles that undergird them—consciousness-raising, integration of content and form, focus on needs and interests, scaffolded tasks—allow for these different emphases. Given the role that innovation can play in genre, genre knowledge, and genre awareness, I turn now to exploring its potential place within academic writing classrooms that aims to support students' development of genre knowledge and/or awareness.

Exploring Genre Innovation in the Classroom

The principles and practices I describe in the following sections are grounded in the contexts of postsecondary writing instruction. Though I hope that many of the activities and assignments might be adaptable to other settings, I also understand that "appropriate" genre instruction can vary rather significantly across contexts and classrooms. Even within the broad contexts I address here—undergraduate and graduate academic writing—there are important differences related to learners' disciplinary participation, content knowledge, target genres, existing genre repertoires, and language backgrounds, to name just a few. Addressing a relatively wide spectrum of learning contexts is, I am aware, somewhat risky. However, what I hope to offer is not a packaged approach but rather a set of more general principles and practices that may provide a starting point for individual teachers.

A second risk posed by this pedagogical discussion is that by describing potential roles for innovation in the classroom, it may unintentionally appear that I am advocating for a focus on innovation *over* convention. To the contrary, in my own classrooms, explorations of convention are given the majority of attention. Most of my teaching has been with multilingual writers who are often contending with unfamiliar genres and unfamiliar social settings in an additional language. They want and can benefit from exposure to and exploration of the socially preferred patterns (or conventions) that mark the genres of their academic lives. Innovation, however, provides an important occasional counter-balance, a way to highlight the flexibility of genre and the ways in which individuals use genres for their own purposes.

Genre Analysis: Convention and Variation

A central aim of genre-based pedagogy has been to demystify genres (and their contexts of use) by fostering awareness of their conventions. Conventions are important for learning because they make visible the frames and schemata of genres, and they offer novice writers a starting place for participating through genres. As we have seen, conventions also are central to variation and innovation. As Bhatia (1997) has noted, "Liberties, innovations, creativities, exploitations, whatever one may choose to call them, are invariably realized within rather than outside the generic boundaries" (p. 367). Familiarity with those boundaries—however unstable and fluid—is therefore crucial ground for novice writers.

Descriptions of genre-based teaching offer numerous examples of activities that enhance students' awareness of genre conventions (Bawarshi, 2003; Devitt, 2004; Hyland, 2007; Johns, 2002b; Paltridge, 2001; Rose & Martin, 2012; Swales, 1990). Various forms of genre analysis—activities that engage students in the explicit analysis of genre texts and contexts—are particularly common. Analysis might focus on identifying rhetorical move structures or patterns of citation use in a mini-corpus of sample texts, helping students to understand how writers demonstrate the importance of their work and build on the work of others within specific genres. Students might also analyze patterns in lexico-grammatical features, such as the use of first-person pronouns or hedges and boosters, leading to discussions of how the language choices within a genre are linked to purpose and social relations. Ethnography-inspired methods, such as interviewing insiders or observing genres as they are carried out (Johns, 1997; Paltridge, 2001; Reiff in Devitt, Bawarshi, & Reiff, 2003), can be of great value in exploring conventions of genre practice and their relations to communities, values, and histories.

Examining genre conventions in these sorts of ways can be very empowering to learners because it helps to demystify the game while also providing them with tools—including a metalanguage—for analyzing and exploring writing. Once conventional patterns become visible, they offer a starting point for writers, a frame for moving forward in expected ways. Through their explorations of text samples, it is also inevitable that students will quickly encounter variation, as no two instances of a genre are identical. As Johns (2008) argues, students need to be familiar with the fact that "texts from genres can, and do, vary, sometimes radically, from situation to situation" (p. 241). Attention to variation encourages a view of genre as dynamic and situated, and, as such, it also may contribute to learners' genre awareness.

Many activities used for noticing conventions can also explicitly examine variation. As students look across sample texts in a genre, they may note not just the similarities but also the distinctions. In an advanced undergraduate classroom, for example, I have asked students to carry out multistep analyses of a genre of their choice, and they begin the project by collecting as many samples of their chosen genre as they can. As they gather samples within single or multiple communities, they fairly quickly notice that variations can occur across communities and contexts or even by individual writers. One student analyzing movie reviews saw that patterns of style and stance varied rather significantly in "public-authored" web reviews versus those by well-known professional reviewers. He also identified important differences in the content of lengthy "film" reviews like those in the *New York Times* compared with very short "movie" reviews that may appear in local newspapers. Other students noted how even within a community or venue, individual users approached the same genre in distinct ways. As students start to link variations to purposes, contexts, communities, and individuals, they begin to develop an understanding of the situated and flexible nature of genres in use. Such an exploration can help to keep at bay the notion that conventions are rules to be followed rather than guides or frames to work within and around.

Examining the variation in genre practice (that is, the processes used to carry out a genre—from research methods to composing practices) can be more challenging but, as many others have suggested, student interviews with experts can be very generative (Johns, 1997; Paltridge, 2001). Students might ask an experienced genre user, for example, to "describe your typical process in writing in this genre, from start to finish." As students compare their interview findings for a single genre, they can see patterns across users as well as individual and community variations. In-class panels of experts (from different fields with different levels of experience) can also be revealing as students together hear a range of perspectives about a single genre or set of genres. In a panel of grant writers for a graduate writing course I taught, for example, students learned about how factors such as research team structures, funding agencies, and research topics all influenced the processes and products of grant proposals. In undergraduate settings, panels of teachers or tutors might be appropriate for revealing a range of expectations for different genres and genre practices.

It can also be worthwhile to ask students to compare possibilities for variation *across* genres, disabusing them of any assumptions that all genres are essentially the same in this regard. In my multistep genre analysis assignment, as students compared their findings with one another, they learned that some genres have relatively less possibility for variation than others—they are, in Bhatia's (2006) words, "conservative" genres. One student studying press releases, for example, found that variation was relatively restricted in that genre, at least in terms of text form. When interviewing expert users, the student was told that there was little room for variation because of the contexts of use and the need for efficient and unambiguous communication. Examples like this can help sensitize students to the different potentials for variation across genres and users—a point that is very applicable to academic genres as well.

A simple way to introduce this concept is to give students a list of genres and to place each on a continuum in terms of their openness to variation, as in the example in Figure 5.2. They can then explore questions of why wide variation is possible, even *valued*, in some genres, such as personal narratives, but more restricted or discouraged in others, such as writing exams. Follow-up discussion might explore the kinds of variation (see Figure 5.1) that might be possible within those different genres. These kinds of discussions can help learners see that all genres vary but that the kinds and ranges of variation may differ.

As they analyze genre samples, either in text form, through discussions with genre users, or even perhaps through observations of genres in action, students may come across examples that seem exceptional and innovative. Even if they do not, they can be asked to look for (or ask an expert to recommend) examples of innovation or even of poorly received deviation. Examining exceptional examples of a genre can help to demonstrate the ways in which individuals take ownership over their texts. Students might consider questions such as, What makes the example unique? What might explain its successful or unsuccessful reception? What aspects of the genre are conventional, and what aspects are atypical?

Figure 5.2. Sample Activity for Exploring Variation across Genres

Some genres may be more open to variation than others. With a partner, place the following genres on the continuum, indicating how "flexible" you think they are.

autobiography, annotated bibliography, book review, business case study report, in-class essay exam, lab report, reading summary

$\longleftarrow \longrightarrow$

low
flexibility

high
flexibility

1. Why do you think some of these genres might be more open to variation than others?

2. For each genre, consider what kinds of variation might be most acceptable for readers.

3. In addition to the genre itself, what other factors might influence how much flexibility a writer has with a text in a given situation?

The set of questions in Figure 5.3, based on the framework outlined at the end of Chapter 3 (see pages 72–94), offer a general heuristic
for guiding students' analyses and discussions of genre innovation,
though they will need to be culled from and adapted for different learners and learning contexts. Students could compare different genres
in terms of their innovation potential, or consider the same genres in
different contexts or by different writers. These kinds of explorations
of innovation can also be valuable for "destabilizing students' genre
theories" (Johns, 2002a) and fostering a situated and rhetorical view of
genre that embraces both convention and variation.

Explorations of genre convention and variation are important in
building a nuanced understanding of genre that can challenge a genre-
as-formula view while still engaging in genre's patterned and typified nature that learners often find so valuable. In the same way that
variable language use challenges the fossilization of an interlanguage
system, variation in genre can challenge an overly stabilized understanding of genre. As students gain more insight into the dynamics of
genre innovation, they engage in metalinguistic awareness and critical
awareness, both of which seem likely to enhance genre awareness. This
focus on meta-awareness also speaks to arguments that classrooms
need to equip students with an understanding of how genres and discourses work before encouraging them to change them. Of course, the
relative balance placed on convention and variation (including innovation) must be determined by individual teachers as they consider
course aims, student goals, and language and writing levels, among
other factors.

Genre Play

Drawing on insights from research on language play, it seems that
there may be some value in providing opportunities for students to
experiment with genres in playful and entertaining ways as well. Such
opportunities may make discourse patterns more "noticeable," can
engage learners in *double-voicing* (which may support sociolinguistic
competence), and may support a complex and dynamic understanding of language and genre. Though no studies that I'm aware of have
systematically examined learners' *genre* play in the classroom, both

Figure 5.3. Guiding Questions for Exploring Innovation Potential in a Genre

---

Community and Users
- How accessible is the community to outsiders and newcomers? How does someone become recognized as a member of the community?
- What kinds of resources (disciplinary knowledge, languages, genres, terminology, technology, etc.) are needed to gain expertise and be considered a community "insider"?
- What marks someone as an expert, novice, or outsider in the community?
- What are the roles of the writers and readers of the genre (e.g., student-teacher, colleague-colleague)? Do they hold roughly equal or different power in the situation?
- Who has more freedom to break from conventional patterns within the genre?
- What are the risks involved in innovation for different writers of the genre?

Innovation, Novelty, and Originality
- What kinds of innovation are valued by community members, and what kinds are discouraged?
- What are some of the reasons that writers may break from convention in this genre and in this community?
- How important are novelty or originality to the community?
- How is novelty defined within the community? What kinds of novelty or originality are considered innovative? What kinds are discouraged?
- Who can create original work? Who, generally, cannot?
- What kinds of resources for innovation (e.g., technologies, languages, collaboration) are available to community members? Do all members have equal access?

Diversity
- How heterogeneous is the community? In what ways?
- How open or closed is the community in interacting with other groups? For example, if the community is an academic discipline or university department, how much does it collaborate with other disciplines or departments? How accepting are the gatekeepers and experts of other communities' ways of doing things?
- To what extent do community members move and collaborate across global, disciplinary, social, and linguistic contexts?

Genre
- How "old" is the genre? What is its history within the community?
- What is at stake with the genre?
- What other people (teachers, editors, peer reviewers, peers) might influence the genre's final form? How much control do they have over the final form?
- How difficult is the genre to learn? What knowledge or background does it require? Is it formally taught, through instruction or guidelines, or learned more informally?
- Is this a relatively conservative genre, or does it seem more open to creative approaches?

Swales (1990, 2004) and Devitt (2004, 2009) have called attention to the importance of playful and humorous manipulations of genre in the classroom, and Hyon (2015) has outlined multiple examples for incorporating genre play into undergraduate writing classes. Their call for such activities is motivated not just by a desire to engage students but also by a concern for enhancing learners' genre awareness. Hyon notes specifically the value of play in drawing attention to convention and the possibilities for manipulating such conventions. Bastian (2015) has similarly argued that a focus on innovation, or disruption, can enhance students' rhetorical awareness, especially when tasks are accompanied by metacognitive reflection. She recounts numerous activities in her own class of undergraduate native-English speakers in which students engaged in unconventional genres and genre-uptakes, reflected on these experiences, and explored the range of resources available to them in using genres in unexpected ways. Many of her students reported feeling that being forced to depart from a conventional process or product led them to "see the FYW classroom as a place where they were learning rather than a place where they were taught."

Although the analysis activities described also work toward the goal of enhanced genre awareness, they place students in an analyst role, as someone looking at genres from the outside. When we ask students to take a hand at manipulating genres themselves, we engage them directly in both the conventions *and* the possibilities for innovation from the role of a writer. Genre play may take a variety of forms, but the examples I share here focus on exploitation of genres through low-stakes but meaningful tasks, often collaborative in nature. The aim of such activities is to engage student-writers with genres in a playful manner but with the goal of building rich genre knowledge and awareness.

Bending and Remixing Genres

Devitt (2004) has described the value of genre bending in a writing classroom, asking students to see how far they might bend conventions before they have created a new genre. I have found that this activity can be too challenging for many novice writers, but the principle behind it is valuable and adaptable. Beginning with more tightly focused activities can help to break down this very open and often intimidating process.

Because many undergraduate writers have been told that they should not use *I* in academic papers, this can be an interesting convention to play with. Students might be given an introductory paragraph that is written in third person and then be asked to rewrite the introduction using first person. As a class they can compare their revisions and discuss the change in style and effect. They can consider which academic genres and communities might avoid the use of first-person pronouns and which might make more frequent use of them—and why.

With graduate student writers, short texts like biostatements can provide good starting points for discussions of genre bending. I have shared a mini-corpus of biostatements with students and asked them to write two biostatements about themselves: one that is prototypical and one that is unusual, bending the conventions in some way. When they present their "bent" text to the class, they also share the context in which they feel the new text may be appropriate. The rest of the class may weigh in too so that students can learn from the different reactions to their manipulated text. Discussions have centered around the risks involved in representing oneself in an unconventional way as well as the potential opportunities for self-expression.

In today's world of rapidly evolving possibilities for design and modality, remixing is a relevant and engaging way to explore genre. Taking two modalities that students are familiar with, I have asked students to examine a PowerPoint version of the Gettysburg Address (Norvig, n.d.) and discuss the bizarre rhetorical shifts that occur when a history-making speech is reduced to bullet-point lists. Students then go through the same process of turning a written text into a short set of presentation slides, drawing from a well-known public text that they are familiar with (from any language). As they remix modes and possibly even linguistic codes, they become sensitized to the resulting shifts in audience, social, purpose, and potential responses.

Exploring Emerging Genres

Emerging technologies and the ubiquity of the internet are constantly giving rise to new possibilities for innovation in written discourse. In academic writing, a variety of genres that are characterized by short, visual presentations of research are increasingly visible, under names such as video abstracts and audio slides. Academic writers, including student writers, are also now engaging in less formal digital genres such as academic blogs, podcasts, and video introductions to their work. Because these genres are often too new to have the kinds of established conventions of research articles, they pose unique challenges to authors. Convention, as we have noted, enables creativity, but in newer genres, writers may have a fuzzier sense of what the creative options are or how to produce a "recognizable" genre. The notion of *recognizability* as a fundamental feature of genre is itself even questionable in many internet genres (Giltrow & Stein, 2009a). This lack of established and visible norms may be both liberating and bewildering for genre newcomers.

In an attempt to explore with students the nature of new genres, I have engaged graduate students with the process of producing video abstracts, a genre that is gaining popularity in the sciences but is still rare in the humanities or social sciences. We began by viewing numerous examples of video abstracts that my students collected, as well as other related and antecedent genres, such as print abstracts, video course descriptions, short TED talks, animated journal articles, and video book summaries. We discussed the exigencies that the video abstract might respond to, the social actions it is used to carry out, and how and when that action might be appropriate. Later, my students produced video abstracts of their seminar projects and shared them with the class. In discussing the challenges of production, they wrestled with the difficulty of creating a text for which they had little experience and few examples and also noted the personal and material influences on their final products. Some students, for example, preferred not to use their face or voice in the video, so they relied on images, short text snippets, and music. One student had prior experience with video technology and was thus able to create a rather snazzy abstract "trailer" followed by a visually creative (and academically interesting) abstract. Other students were wary of spending too much time on producing a video with many bells and whistles and opted for a video of themselves talking through the highlights of their project, an approach they had picked up from several of the examples we had looked at in class. Issues of time, resources, audience, venue, and even the status of the research project (proposed, ongoing, or complete) were some of the many pieces at play in students' available tools for and approaches to this nascent genre. Despite some of these challenges, students noted the value in having to re-package their work and the advantages of being able to incorporate sound, moving images, and personal narrative as resources for sharing their research. While the introduction of a newly emerging genre may not be appropriate in all classes, for students who are ready to contend with more complex aspects of genre, such an activity can be motivating in its creative possibilities and also productive in terms of enhancing genre awareness.

Emerging genres come in a plethora of examples, many of which are well suited to classroom experimentation. Graduate student writers, for instance, can analyze and produce emerging thesis- and dissertation-related genres, such as the three-minute thesis (3MT®) (University of Queensland, n.d.) or a 140-character thesis summary using the Twitter hashtag #tweetyourthesis. Beyond considering the obvious challenges of reducing a multi-year research project to a severely condensed timeframe, they can reflect on what occurs through such radical alterations and what aims might be served by doing so. In undergraduate classrooms, students can similarly tweet their thesis statement or prepare a one-minute video introduction to their paper for a peer. Some kinds of writing, such as personal narratives, might be remediated into digital stories—for example, three- to five-minute personal stories that mix video or still-images with music and an audio narrative. The incorporation of such emerging multimodal genres may allow for increased student motivation and engagement, authentic audiences, and collaborative authorship (Goodwin-Jones, 2012; Hafner, 2013), while also involving students in explorations of genre, convention, and creativity.

It is perhaps worth a reminder that incorporation of emerging genres should be considered with care. For some students and in some courses, such explorations might seem too far afield and less immediately relevant to learners' goals. But even limited engagement with emerging genres can provide an amusing way to explore the fluid and dynamic nature of generic activity as well as the valuable role that conventions can play for writers, providing a possible path in an otherwise unmarked terrain.

New Subject Positions and Identities

An additional benefit of genre play is that it can allow an opportunity for students to adopt new roles within genres, engaging in "semantic language play," such as role play (Tarone, 2000). Taking on different roles, positions, and identities in a genre can allow students opportunities to use genres in new ways while also enhancing their general genre awareness and their genre-specific knowledge. Simple "representational genres"—those that directly assert claims regarding one's identity (Hyland, 2012)—can be a useful place to start. Academic webpages and bios are two examples.

Through his own initiative, one student of mine, Juan, engaged in this kind of genre role play in a high-stakes writing assignment—his course-culminating portfolio in a first-year writing course. Juan was an international student from Argentina in his late twenties at the time of the course. His major was art and design, and he focused all of his writing in the course on this interest, so it was no surprise that his final portfolio reflected not just his identity as an artist but also his playful and creative approach to language.

The portfolio assignment asked students to assemble examples of their work throughout the course, including evidence of revision, and to introduce the collection with a reflective "cover letter" essay. Typically, the cover letter describes the changes and strengths in the student's writing in the course. In its conventional form, there is a strong sense of a teacher audience and a student writer. Juan, however, eschewed these roles for the reader and writer. His cover letter (Figure 5.4) and portfolio did carry out the goals of the assignment, but

Figure 5.4. First-Year Writing Student's Innovative Portfolio Cover Letter

---

Prologue
By Hwan Kong

Continuing my research on the life and work of the acclaimed underground artist Juan Tauber (1978 – 2035) I recently discovered a series of essays, presumably written by him in the winter of 2008, that provide solid examples of the artist as a young person and his early ideas on art. The relevance of this finding is the tangible proof that the artist's learning process through writing determined the change of majors recorded by DePaul University during the spring of 2008; period in which Tauber abandoned the fine arts to focus on digital media. Amongst notes and handouts, the documents found are a series of drafts leading to three final pieces all included in this book. In addition a compilation of six articles responding to publications dealing with art, as it was perceived at the beginning of the 21st century were found. This editorial is a compilation of the most relevant of these documents in order to better explain the development of Tauber's ideas as an artist and his views as a student.

In order to objectively evaluate these pieces, I think it is important to understand Tauber's personal history and context in this particular time period. The material published is arranged in chronological order. It includes two drafts, three final pieces, and a written response to a Laurie Fendrich essay. In this prologue, following a brief explanation of the assignments that shaped this documents, I will attempt to give an insight to the artist's points of view to help the reader better understand Tauber's evolution of ideas about art during this learning process.

A Brief Introduction to the Artist and His Education

As the records show, Juan Tauber was born in 1978 in a small city named Rio Cuarto in the province of Cordoba, Argentina. The artist completed his elementary and secondary education in that town. At the age of 19, presumably fleeing from the law with a much older lover, he moved to the capital of that country, Buenos Aires. There, Tauber enrolled in the UBA (University of Buenos Aires) pursuing a degree in textile design. Three years later, in 1999, Tauber found his passion in the fine arts in a completely unexpected way. He wrote the cover letter from the viewpoint of an art historian who had unearthed early writings from "the acclaimed underground artist Juan Tauber (1978–2035)." The letter, resembling a prologue to an art history book, goes on to describe this writing including the changes evident in it. Juan's actual writing was photo-edited to look like a tattered and crumpled artifact (Figure 5.5), and the entire portfolio was submitted in the form of a dossier. The new positionality from which Juan writes is fascinating not only because of the strong element of play and engagement with the genre, but also because of what he is able to achieve through this exploitation. Taking an outsider view to his own texts allows him a kind of critical distance that actually results in a more persuasive reflection on his writing than is typically found in this genre (where students often feel trapped into telling the teacher what he or she wants to hear). Ultimately, Juan's portfolio won a university-wide writing competition, a testament to its effectiveness.

While Juan's level of genre awareness and willingness to take risks and exploit genres may be exceptional, it demonstrates potential value in activities that engage students in assuming new roles and identities in their writing, giving them a critical and playful distance from dominant norms (Kramsch & Sullivan, 1996). In low-stakes activities, student groups can be given scenarios that ask them to produce a genre (e.g., an opinion piece in a student newspaper or an academic book review) from different subject positions. As they try on these roles and relations, their attention will be drawn to the various rhetorical and linguistic options that are available to them, and they will have the opportunity to practice such options without significant outcomes riding on their success. For students who might feel alienated by particular genres and their norms, such activities also allow the chance to experiment with strategies of negotiation and resistance.

Parody

As discussed in Chapter 3, parody fully engages the tension between convention and innovation in genre. Dating back to *Genre Analysis*, Swales (1990) has advocated for the value of parody in the academic

Figure 5.5. Excerpt from Juan's First-Year Writing Portfolio, Resembling an Aged Historical Document

figure out what's wrong with this piece. I keep on staring at the girl in the drawing: she's young, she's pretty, she's a model. I worked on her face more than anything else. I did a good job, but she's beginning to annoy me. A few minutes later her emptiness continues to annoy me. OK I'm done with her. Very contained, I get up; I walk to the wall and smudge the charcoal on her face with my hand erasing all her features. I feel very brave, without questioning myself and disregarding many hours of work, I erase what I think is the best part of the piece. Now she's facing me, but no longer looking. I walk away from it. All of a sudden the dress seems alive, she has become the object the photographer wanted her to be. All excited I go back to the canvas to clean up a bit of the mess on her face, I finish some little details on the hat and re-draw the meaningless veil over her now faceless face. The piece is finished now. I am just brilliant. I am so proud of this piece; it is probably the best of the series. I varnish it quickly and get ready to take it to the gallery where the rest of the show is already up and a set of screws on the wall is waiting for the new work.

I barely had enough time to mess up my hair and the cab arrives. I am being extremely careful as I carry the unwrapped canvas across the sidewalk. As I get in into the van I requested to comfortably accommodate both the drawing and me, I make sure that the image is straight up. In the rearview mirror I can see that the driver is a healthy man, maybe in his forties. He has kind eyes, a bright smile, and seems to be in a very good mood. After I give him instruction on how to get to the gallery, I encounter an obvious question: "Did you do that?" he says, slightly moving his chin towards the rearview mirror to point at the canvas next to me. Looking out the window behind dark shades, I say "yes, of course" and explain that it will be a part of a solo show. (I really put emphasis on that word, but he seems unmoved. I think that maybe he doesn't know what it means.) " The opening reception is in a couple of days" I continue, "you should come it's gonna be wonderful." I use the mirror to mess up my hair some more and with controlled moves I get my cell phone from my pocket. I check the time;

writing classroom. Parody is in fact a rather sophisticated rhetorical act that relies on knowledge of convention and community. Swales (2004) notes this value, arguing that play may "relax the grip of academic conventions" (p. 249). He points specifically to parody as a "powerful emancipatory device" (p. 250) for writers as they learn to exploit a genre for their own aims. In other words, parodies are not just fun;

they also have the potential for critique and therefore offer opportunities for students to develop their formal, stylistic, and rhetorical awareness.

As shown in the examples of the Sokal Hoax and the "Body Ritual of the Nacirema," described in Chapter 3, parody is typically grounded in critique. To parody a genre, then, blends the emic nature of insider knowledge with the etic perspectives that come with critical distance. When incorporating parody into my own courses, I have found that successful parody requires that students have already explored their target genre in some depth. Without having developed a strong understanding of a genre's form, users, rhetorical actions and strategies, ideologies, and values, they are challenged to exploit generic conventions in a meaningful and purposeful way. Therefore, parody will be most appropriate in classes in which students spend a fair amount of time building their knowledge of a specific genre.

Students can be aided in producing parodies by looking first at examples and discussing how they are able to distinguish the parody from the sincere examples. Visual parodies—such as those of advertisements or company logos—are an effective way to introduce the concept to students who may not be familiar with it. Students may then discuss the strategies that are used for parody, including exaggeration or violation of conventions, inclusion of unexpected or even taboo content, or adopting uncommon stances. Though short texts or parts of texts—such as academic paper titles, dissertation acknowledgements, or introductions—provide appropriate starting points, parodying a longer genre, especially one that plays an important role in students' lives, could be a valuable activity in some contexts.

Critique and Ownership

As described in Chapter 3, genre innovation is at times motivated by a desire to resist or critique dominant discourses. This kind of innovation may use strategies like parody or satire, but can also purposefully depart from expected conventions as a way of taking a critical stance (Dietel-McLaughlin, 2009). A critical approach to genre in the classroom may examine the inherent power structures in genre and engage learners in the possibilities for and limitations to challenging those structures in their writing. Devitt (2009), for instance, advocates teaching critical genre awareness, the goal of which is "a conscious attention to genres and their potential influences on people and the ability to consider acting differently within genres" (p. 347). This kind of approach can help to address concerns about the reproduction of social power through genres and may also support the call for the critical awareness of power and privilege that scholars like Kubota (2012) have advocated. As Swales (2004) has put it, "We are never free of our institutional roles, but becoming more aware of their constraints somehow loosens their grip" (p. 252).

Genre critique may be guided through analysis of sample texts or interviews with insiders, especially perhaps relative newcomers who are often particularly aware of the ideologies that adhere to genres. While the genres appropriate for critique will depend on the course, context, and students, educational genres may be especially effective for introducing critical analysis in a school setting. Course syllabi and course or instructor evaluations, for example, are ripe for critique among undergraduates, as they position students in relatively limited roles within the institution. I have found that students in the United States become especially engaged in critique of course evaluation forms, as they participate in this genre multiple times each semester throughout their time at university, and it provides an illustration of the power of genres within social (and economic) systems. Other such genres might include high-stakes writing placement exams or even assignment guidelines from courses students are concurrently enrolled in. Students may examine how they are positioned within these writing activities and how their own identities and values might be constrained by the ecosocial environment. What are the expectations and the "culturally available options" (Hyland, 2012) within this context? What are the opportunities for resistance or exploitation of these genres?

While challenging dominant forms can be risky in many student-produced genres, writers may find other ways to manipulate the task to serve their own needs. The immigrant and international students in Harklau's (2000) and Leki's (1995) research, for instance, learned that invoking particular identities—as a stereotypical hard-working immigrant or as a student with special status and transnational knowledge—afforded them some symbolic capital and allowed them to negotiate assignments in ways that were well received by their instructors. Classroom discussions might help build students' strategies for identifying theses kinds of culturally available options for manipulating genres.

Finally, the ubiquitous use of English as a language of international scholarship may be an additional aspect of genre that is ripe for critique in academic settings, with both undergraduate and graduate student populations. Once students begin to see how genres reflect interests of certain people (and not others), they may also consider available options for asserting their own goals as well as possibilities for resisting dominant norms, if and when they wish to.

A word of caution, though, is perhaps necessary. While critique is a common goal in U.S. undergraduate education, especially in the first-year writing curriculum, it is neither a universal value nor a universally appropriate classroom aim. Thinking back to my experiences teaching ESP to Japanese researchers at a multinational company's headquarters in Japan, I can imagine numerous ways in which I *could have* had students critique the genres that held great power over them. They were required to use English exclusively, despite being in Japan, and they had to produce nearly all of their writing within a limited range of four different types of company reports, all of which exuded the ideologies of fast-paced, time-efficient, bottom-line corporate America. The stakes were high as well. The company spent large amounts of money on English language training, investing in these workers' multilingualism, and promotion within the company was dependent on high levels of English proficiency. While there is much that I and my students could have critiqued, it would not have been without risk.

In the end, I opted for occasional genre play, including role play, as a way to raise awareness of values and potential inequities, but I never directly discussed with students the power of the genres they worked in and their own roles—and mine—within that system. On the other hand, my colleagues and I designed writing courses that paid limited attention to the use of standardized forms of American English, rarely correcting uses of Japanese English and indeed often working with examples of model texts that made extensive use of localized lexical and grammatical features; instead, we emphasized the preferred rhetorical forms of the company report and memo types.

It is likely that if I found myself in the same job today, I would be bolder and would find subtle ways to integrate a more critical awareness of genre. Yet, as Paltridge (2001) notes, critique of genre requires a certain level of language proficiency, and not all of my students were at such a level. Critique also requires a fair degree of knowledge about a genre's community of users and complicated contexts of use; in some cases, students may be too far removed from these communities and contexts to develop this kind of knowledge within the confines of a writing classroom. The larger point here is that the extent to which an individual instructor and her students may find critique appropriate and productive within a learning environment will vary considerably—and this variation is also an important component of understanding genre innovation as part of a larger ecosocial system. Innovation for the purpose of challenging dominant practices is not to be treated lightly. As shared earlier, Matsuda and Matsuda's (2010) principles for teaching writing from a WE perspective offer useful guidelines here:

1. Teach the dominant language forms and functions.
2. Teach the non-dominant language forms and functions.
3. Teach the boundary between what works and what does not work.
4. Teach the principles and strategies of discourse negotiation.
5. Teach the risks involved in using deviational features.

Examining examples of normative and subversive texts (and the often fuzzy boundaries between these) can lead to discussions of what kinds of transgressions are possible and most effective, by whom, and in what genres.

Learner-Appropriate Pedagogy

To return to a point made earlier, individual teachers will need to determine the appropriate balance among convention, variation, and innovation within their writing classrooms. While experienced writers may value and benefit from engagement in many of the practices described, novice writers may be better served by greater attention to convention augmented by a more limited role for innovation. Exploration of genre variation is valuable in any classroom, as it helps to challenge views of genre as a template while still focusing on community options and expectations.

Language proficiency and prior genre experience in other languages are important factors as well. In a longitudinal study of three international students writing in English as an additional language, Myles and Artemeva (2014) found that the writers perceived very limited connection between their prior experiences writing in L1 academic genres and those they encountered at a Canadian university. This perception that their English academic writing was "totally different" from their L1 academic writing may have contributed to the students' views of themselves as novice or inexperienced writers in English—despite seeing themselves as strong academic writers in their first languages. Notably, these students also reported different prior genre experience than the first-year U.S. undergraduates in Reiff and Bawarshi's (2011) study. Fiction, poetry, and five-paragraph essays, for example, were very familiar to the U.S. students but the international students had limited or no experience with these genres. Given the differences in students' prior experiences and comfort level with English academic genres, Myles and Artemeva argue that a scaffolded approach to academic writing instruction may be most beneficial for some students. They describe this approach as initially focusing on models in order to familiarize students with specific genres of importance, then, as students gain experience and comfort with English academic writing, focusing on raising their genre awareness and, eventually, critical awareness of academic genres.

The scaffolded approach described here echoes arguments made by Johns (2011) that novice writers benefit from more guided support than is found in many rhetorically focused genre pedagogies. The approach resonates with my own experience as well. When researching a graduate-level writing course with very advanced multilingual students, for example, it seemed to me that the broad heuristic used in the class for analyzing a genre's form, context, practice, and ideologies was of little value to students. Students were asked to contend with too much information at once and were unable to see the purpose and relevance to their writing development (see Tardy, 2009, and Tardy in Johns et al., 2006). For many students, attending specifically to linguistic and rhetorical patterns first helps them to build the necessary schemata and frames for their own generic practices; indeed, many studies have found the use of models and sample texts to provide a valuable learning strategy for writers (Tardy, 2006). Even when a classroom focuses on prototypical examples, however, students can benefit from exposure to variation and innovation. Similarly, activities that aim toward raising more general genre awareness can be integrated gradually and with increasing complexity.

In addition to a scaffolded approach to awareness-raising, teachers should consider how specific tasks and assignments are sequenced within the classroom. For instance, Devitt (2009) describes a cycle of analysis, production, critique, and change. I have had some success with a similarly sequenced set of tasks in undergraduate writing courses in which students move through these steps with a genre of their choice:

1. analysis of the genre's purposes, users, and places of use
2. analysis of rhetorical moves
3. analysis of lexico-grammatical patterns of use
4. creation of a prototypical instance of the genre
5. interviews with expert users on the genre practices and uses
6. creation of a new version of the text produced in Step 4, written for a new audience or forum
7. analysis of the sets and systems in which the target genre exists
8. creation of a text that plays with some of the conventions, but in a way that users might find effective
9. critical genre analysis
10. creation of a parody of the genre

This spiraled approach integrates analysis and production as well as convention and variation (and innovation) throughout. Sample prompts for Steps 4, 6, 8, and 10 are found in Figure 5.6, and these can be adapted as appropriate for different learners and courses. My students inevitably find the creation of the subtly bent texts (Step 8) to be the most challenging. Most often, they struggle with bending or flouting a genre in ways that are rhetorically effective and do not result in a parody. The assignment provides an opportunity, as well, to think

Figure 5.6. Sample Writing Prompts for Sequenced Genre Exploration

Genre Prototype Based on your analyses of your target genre, create a prototypical example of the genre, mimicking the most common features of the genre that you have identified so far. If the genre you analyzed is very long, you may mimic just part of it here. If your genre is very short (e.g., a horoscope), produce several examples.
Genre Rewrite Rewrite your genre prototype for a different audience or forum. For instance, if your original text was a research article (reporting on a research study), you might write a short news story about the research for a popular magazine. You may choose to write in the role of the original author, or as someone else who is summarizing the original text for a general audience. As you rewrite your text for this new audience and forum, you will need to consider what kinds of changes are necessary to content, organization, language use and style, reader-writer roles, length, and formatting. These shifts will show evidence of your understanding of the changes that result from new contexts of writing.
Genre Bending Bend your target genre in some way so that your text is not a prototypical example but is still recognizable as falling within the genre. Imagine a specific rhetorical context in which your "bent" text might be used, and consider how you can play with the genre's form, content, or practices to produce a non-prototypical text *that would still be considered effective by community members*. If the genre you analyzed is very long, you may compose just part of it here; if your genre is very short, produce several examples, bending it in different ways in each example.
Genre Parody Based on your critical genre analysis, create a parody of your target genre. The parody should poke fun at the genre in a way that critiques some aspect of it while still being recognizable as *a parody of* your selected genre. If the genre you analyzed is very long, you may parody just part of it here; if your genre is very short (e.g., a horoscope), produce several parody examples.

about convention, variation, and innovation in ways that go beyond textual form.

Ultimately, the success of the students' genre-texts in this sequence is not really the aim so much as the opportunity to experiment with generic forms, content, and practices, and to explore their available options within communities and genres. They may be completed as ungraded and/or collaborative in-class activities, for example, or they might be compiled at the end of the course into a genre portfolio that also includes an introduction reflecting on the learner's choices. Teachers will also need to determine what will be assessed (students' genre awareness, their ability to use and exploit genre conventions, or a combination?) and how (written reflections, formal papers, in-class activities, genre portfolios).

This sequence is particularly geared toward building students' genre awareness, but it could be adapted for courses that are more concerned with the acquisition of specific genres—as in an ESP/EAP course or an advanced Writing in the Disciplines course. Of key importance is acknowledging the roles of both convention and innovation in genre, engaging students with the tension that is always at play in social uses of language. Teachers can help students consider not just the available options, but also how such options shift for different users, contexts, and genres, and how convention, variation, and innovation may be evaluated within the systems in which they are produced and received. To keep the complexities of genre in sight, however, we may need to begin by paring things down and then gradually destabilizing and complicating students' ever-evolving genre theories.

The primary goal of this chapter was to demonstrate the role that genre innovation can play in the academic writing classroom as a valuable means of consciousness-raising that can, ultimately, contribute to students' genre awareness and to their genre-specific knowledge. I have not attempted to provide a packaged pedagogy or a universal approach to incorporating innovation because doing so would fly in the face of much of what we know about both genre and teaching as highly localized and situated endeavors. Nevertheless, the types of practices I've described offer some examples of ways in which teachers can engage students, as analysts and producers of genres, in the productive tensions between genre convention and innovation. By drawing attention to the innovation potential of genre, teachers can work against a tendency for classroom writing to reinforce static views of academic genres.

One question that might arise is whether activities like these are only appropriate for more advanced writers and language users. While many activities in this chapter assume a fairly high level of language proficiency, in most cases, they can be adapted for different learners. Use of students' multiple language resources can also be incorporated to a greater degree, especially in classrooms in which students share linguistics codes (such as foreign language classrooms). Comparisons of innovative examples of a genre across languages can engage students in both metalinguistic awareness and critical awareness and can perhaps lead to an even more robust *multilingual* genre awareness.

It may also be worth re-stating that issues of risk, power, and privilege cannot be peripheral to discussions of genre innovation. As Heng Hartse and Kubota (2014) wisely caution:

> Advocating for innovative textual practices in our academic community might enhance our own academic profiles but may create little practical benefit for scholars struggling to publish [or, presumably, students developing as writers]. Exercising hyper-self-reflexivity toward our own privilege of being able to manipulate academic conventions and simultaneously propose a utopian vision perhaps leads us to consider a double edged approach to contextually negotiating lexicogrammatical accuracy in academic writing. (p. 80)

Such negotiation—whether it occurs in classrooms or research groups, with teachers, advisors, or editors—can also not be limited to those in less powerful roles but must include an openness toward variation from those in positions of privilege as well.

This last point raises another important consideration for genre-based pedagogy. The practices outlined in this chapter rely on teachers' genre awareness, or their understanding of genre as rhetorical, situated, and dynamic. These approaches also situate teachers not just as writing teachers but also as language teachers (regardless of the language backgrounds of students) and as teachers of discourse and discourse analysis. In many contexts, such roles and backgrounds cannot be assumed and may even be resisted. Many of the activities described here, then, may also have a place in the professional development of writing teachers, working toward the goal of helping teachers establish "a systematic means of describing texts and of making our students' control over them more achievable" (Hyland, 2007, p. 163).

Chapter 6

The Centrality of Genre Innovation

"If academic writing in general is not to become a sterile, formula-oriented activity, we have to encourage individual creativity in writing. It is the tension between received conventions and the innovative spirit of the individual that produces good writing in academic disciplines as well as in creative literature."

—*Kachru, 1997, p. 344*

"While writing, like dancing, allows for creativity and the unexpected, established patterns often form the basis of any variations."

—*Hyland, 2007, p. 150*

These quotes highlight a tension that I have found myself struggling with throughout this book. Is genre innovation an individual, creative endeavor, or is inextricably tied to social systems? The answer is, of course, both. I admit that when I started my exploration of genre innovation, I was primarily motivated by a desire to understand the pragmatic capaciousness of genre than to encourage individual creativity—though the more I read, the more convinced I became of the value in individual manipulations of genre. The issues I've explored in the previous chapters are marked somewhat by these tensions as well. Innovation is about using genres in a rhetorically savvy way, exploiting genres for self-expression, and resisting or changing genres and the systems of power they reflect and reinforce. It is the potential for these multiple opportunities that makes genre innovation so interesting and so worthy of investigation. In essence, the argument that I have attempted to lay out in this book includes three main claims:

1. Genres encompass convention and innovation.
2. Genre knowledge encompasses convention and innovation.
3. Genre innovation has a role to play in the academic writing classroom.

In this final chapter, then, I will review the basic principles of this argument and conclude by outlining some fruitful lines for continued exploration of genre innovation.

A Case for Genre Innovation

Genres Encompass Convention and Innovation

That genres are marked by both convention and innovation is not a new argument but rather is fundamental to understanding genre. Nevertheless, it seems fair to say that much more attention has been paid to convention than to its more idiosyncratic counterpart. This is perhaps because genre is most obviously recognizable through conventions. Or perhaps our attention to convention is driven by the fact that genre has largely been of pedagogical interest in disciplines like applied linguistics, rhetoric and composition, and education. An ability to identify and understand norms—whether they be related to forms or social practices—is, after all, remarkably useful for developing writers.

But while convention is the deserved center of attention for most genre scholarship, knowing more about innovation can certainly contribute to our theories of genre. There is evidence, as well, that innovation may be increasingly important to understand in an era in which language is characterized as both local and mobile (Blommaert, 2010; Pennycook, 2012), so that we write for and with people who are intimately connected to our immediate environments and with whom we share little local knowledge. As our texts—and their readers—move across such spaces, notions of convention and innovation become problematized and less predictable. What is conventional in one locale may become innovative or deviant in another. And the people and places involved matter, as they bring with them perceptions of symbolic power and social relations, both of which play a role in "reading" genres. More robust understandings of genre innovation may also be necessary as we contend with the emerging and rapidly evolving genres made possible by new technologies. The tools for understanding innovation outlined in Chapter 2 offer a starting place but may be insufficient for capturing the highly distributed but also immediately local nature of many digital genres. And we may need to understand better how convention operates in these genres before we can fully address the question of innovation.

Genre Knowledge Encompasses Convention and Innovation

One clear theme in genre scholarship is that expert users can and do exploit, play with, and change genres. It would seem, then, that an understanding of genre innovation is part of expert genre knowledge. Experts are not manipulated by genres but rather know how to use them for their own purposes in different settings. Situating genre innovation within genre knowledge, however, also implores us to consider innovation as related to *social action,* not simply to text form. In other words, if genre is considered to be a social and rhetorical category, and genre knowledge includes knowledge of textual forms, rhetorical strategies, epistemologies, ideologies, sociopolitics, content, and situated practices, then innovation, like convention, does not occur solely at the level of form. As illustrated in Chapters 3 and 4, innovation in academic genres can be found in research practices, composing practices, and research questions and analysis, to name just a few examples. Understanding innovation potential in these various dimensions of genre allows us to see the range of opportunities available to writers for exploiting and even flouting genres.

Moreover, such a view of innovation necessitates an understanding of the social and ecological systems in which genres are produced, used, read, and evaluated. If genres are a social practice, they are not inherently boring, creative, deviant, efficient, or innovative. Rather, such judgments are assigned to genres by people; once again, a genre text may be innovative in one circumstance and deviant or even conventional in another. There also may be distinct opportunities for innovation within different ecosocial systems. Across academic disciplines, for example, we may find a wide range of approaches to and values of innovation. Such variations are also likely to be found across time periods, geographic and institutional locations, and individual users.

Genre Innovation Has a Role to Play in the Academic Writing Classroom

This final component of my argument may be the most contentious, though, in the end, it is by no means a radical shift to prevailing thoughts on genre-based pedagogy. If we concede that innovation is part of genre knowledge and also genre awareness, then it seems that it does have a role to play in a writing classroom that aims to develop students' understandings of genre. In many ways, existing approaches to genre-based teaching already do this by drawing students' attention to the importance of variation in genres. But given the tendency for learners to understand writing in relatively static ways—an understanding that is increasingly reinforced by the looming presence of high-stakes, standardized writing tests—perhaps we need to push a bit further. Attention to innovation, alongside convention, may have great value in challenging perceptions of genres as formulas, even ones that have some flexibility. Innovation may reposition genres as springboards, starting points, or potential pathways. Such an approach, however, comes with an important caveat: Explorations of innovation must take seriously the ecosocial systems in which innovations occur and are judged. Linguistic and rhetorical transgressions, for example, may be very effective when carried out by leading scholars but are unlikely to be received similarly in a student text. Alternative discourses may be highly effective in a student's personal essay but would likely be judged more harshly in the same student's business case study report.

Insights from research on language play and arguments for new paradigms of pluricentric norms can contribute to genre-based pedagogy by offering tools for genre play and experimentation. Valuably, such playful manipulation of genres draws students' attention to convention and the potentials for innovation. Analysis of variation and innovation can raise students' critical consciousness of genre, contributing to the important aim of destabilizing and enhancing their genre awareness. Such an approach might help to flip from a view of genres as things to be learned to a view of genre as things to exploit—working within established and recognizable conventions. And again, it is here where notes of caution are especially important. Adapting a sociocultural view of creativity to the classroom, when teachers ask students to play with genres, we cannot skim over the question of how such experimentations might be received in different environments. Instead, these questions become even more essential.

Looking Ahead

While this book has offered empirical and pedagogical tools for understanding genre innovation, there is much more to be explored. Studies of genre innovation that examine the ecosocial systems in which genres are produced, used, and evaluated could contribute a great deal. It would be valuable, for example, to know more about the variations across disciplinary communities but also about the contested ways in which norm-departures are received *within* a community. Ethnographically oriented research would be particularly useful in understanding how roles, relations, available resources, and power structures, for example, play out in these processes. Longitudinal studies of writers would also be very valuable in exploring how attempts to manipulate or exploit genres might develop in relation to knowledge of convention, disciplinary ways of knowing, and disciplinary identities. When newcomers successfully innovate, what knowledge and resources do they draw upon? How does this compare to the innovations of those with more experience and expertise? What kinds of innovation are most and least successful for novices?

Though research into language play is still limited, the work that has been done suggests potential value in language play and, by extension, genre play. Studies of classroom learning that includes genre play might look at the extent to which it engages noticing and genre awareness. Studies that look at genre play by experts and newcomers (including students) might also explore how it relates to their knowledge of the specific genre, including the social environments of use. Related to this, we need to know more about the relationships among genre play, genre knowledge, and language and writing proficiency. For example, is a certain level of proficiency needed for writers to learn through play? Again, existing studies in language play may provide some useful starting points for such inquiry.

Another area of direct relevance to genre-based writing instruction that deserves more attention is assessment. Between standardized, high-stakes writing tests and timed written exams in university classrooms, much student writing takes place in these highly constrained and often rigid genres. The kinds of innovation valued in these contexts might be very distinct (is it originality? a confident voice?) and is worthy of more exploration. In addition, the emphasis placed on exam writing in tests like the College English Test (CET) in China or the TOEFL®—along with the growing use of machine scoring—may serve to reinforce template-like conceptions of writing for many students, perhaps lending some added value to the exploration of variation and innovation in writing classrooms.

Given the current interest in genre and its role in writing instruction, it is also surprising how little research has examined genre-based pedagogy from teachers' perspectives. Because of concerns that a genre-based approach may default to teaching static formulas, teacher education and teacher knowledge would seem to be important areas of focus. Yet, research to date has largely overlooked questions regarding the kinds of knowledge and resources that teacher might need to implement such an approach in effective ways, with the exception of work in systemic functional linguistics (SFL)–oriented genre pedagogy within elementary and secondary school contexts (e.g., de Oliveira & Lan, 2014; Gebhard & Harman, 2011; Rose & Martin, 2012).

In U.S. undergraduate writing instruction, responsible for teaching writing to large numbers of domestic and international students, there has been no serious attention given to what teachers need to know in order to support students' genre awareness—despite an increasing presence of the term *genre* in the first-year writing textbook market. This lack of attention is especially concerning because a great many teachers in this context are graduate students or contingent faculty with disciplinary backgrounds in literature or creative writing rather than writing studies or applied linguistics. In other words, their exposure to genre theory and pedagogy is typically limited to whatever is taught in practicum courses or teacher development workshops. Even in EAP/ESP contexts, where training in TESOL and applied linguistics is fairly common, teachers may not be familiar with genre theory or pedagogy. Without such backgrounds, teachers may essentially understand genres as text types and may inadvertently present them to students as relatively static forms. Attention to genre convention, variation, and innovation in teacher support programs may therefore be of great value as a means of raising *teachers'* genre awareness. Research might examine how such support influences teachers' knowledge and practices. Studies of teachers' experiences in the classroom could enhance our understanding of the challenges that teachers face in implementing genre-based pedagogies, even when the teachers themselves have a strong grasp of related theories and practices.

Finally, I should note two important aspects of genre innovation that this book has not addressed, at least in any substantive way. First is the role of innovation in genre change. While this book has looked at individual instances of innovation, studies examining innovation in single fields or genres over time may be able to shed light on its role in contributing to genre change. Historical studies might also be able to provide insight into how judgments of innovation are situated in place *and time*. What are some of the rhetorical elements that might make a deviation successful at one point in time but not another?

Another important area of inquiry that I've given little space to here is the role of innovation in today's digital age. Though it often seems that digital genres change more rapidly than print genres, research might explore whether there are specific characteristics of these genres—perhaps related to audience, collaboration, or distribution—that make them more amenable to innovation and change, or whether their apparently accelerated evolution simply relates to the speeds of technological innovation. Studies that examine how roles and relations, including perceptions of symbolic capital, play out in digital genres are also important to understanding innovation. Maurer's (2009) analysis of homeless blogs, for instance, demonstrates how responses to innovation in this genre are still shaped within larger social structures of power. The power to write for the world does not necessarily translate into power to shape how the world might perceive us. Collections like Giltrow and Stein's (2009b) have begun to explore the unique dynamics of digital genres, but there is much more to be done.

In the end, a goal of this book has been to momentarily shift our gaze from convention to variation and innovation as a way to push our understanding of genres and genre-oriented pedagogy, a goal perhaps made more pressing in today's mobile, hypermediated, and "glocal" world. By looking specifically at innovative variation, I have tried to gain some insight into the flux in genres and how that flux is deeply embedded in the actions, judgments, and social relations of people. Without the potential to bend, flout, disrupt, resist, parody, critique, and transform the genres that regulate communication, they become static and insufficient tools for human communication. Innovation is, by definition, unusual, but the possibility for innovation is central to genre.

REFERENCES

Allison, D. (2004). Creativity, students' academic writing, and EAP: Exploring comments on writing in an English language degree program. *Journal of English for Academic Purposes, 3*(1), 191–209.

Amabile, T. M. (1982). Social psychology of creativity: A consensual assessment technique. *Journal of Personality and Social Psychology, 43*(5), 997–1013.

Amabile, T. M. (1988). A model of creativity and innovation in organizations. *Research in Organizational Behavior, 10,* 123–167.

American Comparative Literature Association. (n.d.) ACL(x) rationale. Retrieved from www.complit.la.psu.edu/aclx/rationale.html

Ashmore, M. (1989). *The reflexive thesis: Wrighting sociology of scientific knowledge.* Chicago: University of Chicago Press.

Baker, W., & Eggington, W. G. (1999). Bilingual creativity, multidimensional analysis, and world Englishes. *World Englishes, 18*(3), 343–358.

Bakhtin, M. M. (1968). *Rabelais and his world* (H. Iswolskz, Trans. 1963). Bloomington: Indiana University Press.

Bakhtin, M. M. (1981). *The dialogic imagination: Four essays* (M. Holquist, Ed., C. Emerson & M. Holquist, Trans.). Austin: University of Texas Press.

Bakhtin, M. M. (1986). *Speech genres and other late essays* (C. Emerson & M. Holquist, Eds. & Trans.). Austin: University of Texas Press.

Baldauf, R. B., Jr., & Jernudd, B. H. (1983a). Language of publications as a variable in scientific communications. *Australian Review of Applied Linguistics, 6,* 97–108.

Baldauf, R. B., Jr., & Jernudd, B. H. (1983b). Language use patterns in the fisheries periodical literature. *Scientometrics, 5,* 245–255.

Bamgboṣe, A. (1998). Torn between the norms: Innovations in world Englishes. *World Englishes, 17*(1), 1–14.

Bastian, H. (2015). Capturing individual uptake: Toward a disruptive research methodology. *Composition Forum, 31.* Retrieved from www.compositionforum.com/issue/31/individual-uptake.php

Bawarshi, A. S. (2003). *Genre and the invention of the writer: Reconsidering the place of invention in composition.* Logan: Utah State University Press.

Bazerman, C. (1988). *Shaping written knowledge: The genre and activity of the experimental article in science.* Madison: University of Wisconsin Press.

177

Beaufort, A. (2004). Developmental gains of a history major: A case for building a theory of disciplinary writing expertise. *Research in the Teaching of English, 30,* 136–185.

Becher, T., & Trowler, P. R. (2001). *Academic tribes and territories* (2nd ed.). New York: SRHE and Open University Press.

Belcher, D. D. (1997). An argument for nonadversarial argumentation: On the relevance of the feminist critique of academic discourse to L2 writing pedagogy. *Journal of Second Language Writing, 6,* 1–21.

Belcher, D. D. (2007). Seeking acceptance in an English-only research world. *Journal of Second Language Writing, 16,* 1–22.

Belcher, D. D. (2009). How research space is created in a diverse research world. *Journal of Second Language Writing, 16,* 1–22.

Belcher, D. D., & Hirvela, A. (2005). Writing the qualitative dissertation: What motivates and sustains commitment to a fuzzy genre? *Journal of English for Academic Purposes, 4*(3), 187–205.

Belz, J. A., & Reinhardt, J. (2004). Aspects of advanced foreign language proficiency: Internet-mediated German language play. *International Journal of Applied Linguistics, 14*(3), 324–362.

Benesch, S. (2001). *Critical English for academic purposes.* Mahwah, NJ: Lawrence Erlbaum.

Berkenkotter, C., & Huckin, T. (1995). *Genre knowledge in disciplinary communication.* Mahwah, NJ: Lawrence Erlbaum.

Berkenkotter, C., Huckin, T. N., & Ackerman, J. (1988). Conventions, conversations, and certainty: Case study of a student in a rhetoric Ph.D. program. *Research in the Teaching of English, 22*(1), 9–44.

Bhatia, V. K. (1993). *Analysing genre: Language use in professional settings.* London: Longman.

Bhatia, V. K. (1997). The power and politics of genre. *World Englishes, 16*(3), 359–371.

Bhatia, V. K. (1999). Integrating products, processes, purposes and participants in professional writing. In C. N. Candlin & K. Hyland (Eds.), *Writing: Texts, processes and practices* (pp. 21–39). New York: Longman.

Bhatia, V. K. (2004). *Worlds of written discourse: A genre-based view.* New York: Continuum.

Bhatia, V. K. (2006). Genres and styles in world Englishes. In B. B. Kachru, Y. Kachru, & C. Nelson (Eds.), *The handbook of world Englishes* (pp. 386–399). Malden, MA: Wiley-Blackwell.

Bhatt, R. M. (2001). World Englishes. *Annual Review of Anthropology, 30,* 527–550.

Bizzell, P. (2002). The intellectual work of "mixed" forms of academic discourses. In C. Schroeder, H. Fox, & P. Bizzell (Eds.), *ALT/DIS: Alternative discourses and the academy* (pp. 1–10). Portsmouth, NH: Boynton/Cook Heinemann.

Blommaert, J. (2005). *Discourse*. Cambridge, U.K.: Cambridge University Press.

Blommaert, J. (2010). *The sociolinguistics of globalization*. Cambridge, U.K.: Cambridge University Press.

Bourdieu, P. (1991). *Language and symbolic power* (J. B. Thompson, Ed., G. Raymond & M. Adamson, Trans.). Cambridge, MA: Harvard University Press.

Broner, M. A., & Tarone, E. E. (2000). Language play in immersion classroom discourse: Some suggestions for language teaching. *Australian Review of Applied Linguistics, 16*, 121–133.

Broner, M. A., & Tarone, E. E. (2001). Is it fun? Language play in a fifth-grade Spanish immersion classroom. *The Modern Language Journal, 85*(3), 363–379.

Burrough-Boenisch, J. (2003). Shapers of published NNS research articles. *Journal of Second Language Writing, 12*, 223–243.

Bushnell, C. (2008). 'Lego my keego!': An analysis of language play in beginning Japanese as a foreign language classroom. *Applied Linguistics, 30*(1), 49–69.

California State University, Bakersfield. (2006). *Rubric packet*. Retrieved from www.csub.edu/TLC/options/resources/handouts/Rubric_Packet_Jan06.pdf

Canagarajah, A. S. (1996). "Nondiscursive" requirements in academic publishing, material resources of periphery scholars, and the politics of knowledge production. *Written Communication, 13*, 435–472.

Canagarajah, A. S. (2002). *A geopolitics of academic writing*. Pittsburgh, PA: University of Pittsburgh Press.

Canagarajah, A. S. (2006a). The place of world Englishes in composition: Pluralization continued. *College Composition and Communication, 57*(4), 586–619.

Canagarajah, A. S. (2006b). Toward a writing pedagogy of shuttling between languages: Learning from multilingual writers. *College English, 68*(6), 589–604.

Canagarajah, A. S. (2013). *Translingual practice: Global Englishes and cosmopolitan relations*. London: Routledge.

Canagarajah, A. S., & Lee, E. (2014). Negotiating alternative discourses in academic writing and publishing: Risks with hybridity. In L. Thesen & L. Cooper (Eds.), *Risk in academic writing: Postgraduate students, their teachers and the making of knowledge* (pp. 59–99). Bristol, U.K.: Multilingual Matters.

Carter, R. (2004). *Language and creativity: The art of common talk*. London: Routledge.

Carter, R. (2007). Response to special issue of *Applied Linguistics* devoted to *Language Creativity in Everyday Contexts*. *Applied Linguistics, 28*(4), 597–608.

Casanave, C. P. (2002). *Writing games: Multicultural case studies of academic literacy practices in higher education*. Mahwah, NJ: Lawrence Erlbaum.

Casanave, C. P. (2010). Taking risks? A case study of three doctoral students writing qualitative dissertations at an American university in Japan. *Journal of Second Language Writing, 19*(1), 1–16.

Cekaite, A., & Aronsson, K. (2005). Language play, a collaborative resource in children's L2 learning. *Applied Linguistics, 26*(2), 169–191.

Cheng, A. (2007). Transferring generic features and recontextualizing genre awareness: Understanding writing performance in the ESP genre-based literacy framework. *English for Specific Purposes, 26,* 287–307.

Cheng, A. (2011). Language features as the pathways to genre: Students' attention to non-prototypical features and its implications. *Journal of Second Language Writing, 20,* 69–82.

Cherry, R. D. (1998). Ethos versus persona: Self-representation in written discourse. *Written Communication, 15*(3), 384–410.

Cook, G. (1994). *Discourse and literature.* Oxford, U.K.: Oxford University Press.

Cook, G. (2000). *Language play, language learning.* Oxford, U.K.: Oxford University Press.

Crystal, D. (1998). *Language play.* Chicago: University of Chicago Press.

Csikszentmihalyi, M. (1996). *Creativity: Flow and the psychology of discovery and invention.* New York: Harper Collins.

Csikszentmihalyi, M. (1999). Implications of a systems perspective for the study of creativity. In R. J. Sternberg (Ed.), *Handbook of creativity* (pp. 313–335). Cambridge, U.K.: Cambridge University Press.

Cummins, J. (2007). Rethinking monolingual instructional strategies in multilingual classrooms. *Canadian Journal of Applied Linguistics, 10*(2), 221–240.

Cummins, J. (2009). Multilingualism in the English-language classroom: Pedagogical considerations. *TESOL Quarterly, 43*(2), 317–321.

de Oliveira, L. C., & Lan, S.-W. (2014). Writing science in an upper elementary classroom: A genre-based approach to teaching English language learners. *Journal of Second Language Writing, 25,* 23–39.

Devitt, A. J. (2004). *Writing genres.* Carbondale: Southern Illinois University Press.

Devitt, A. J. (2009). Teaching critical genre awareness. In C. Bazerman, A. Bonini, & D. Figueiredo (Eds.), *Genre in a changing world: Perspectives on writing* (pp. 337–351). West Lafayette, IN: Parlor Press.

Devitt, A. J. (2011, April). *Creating within genres: How genre metaphors shape student innovation.* Paper presented at the Conference on College Composition and Communication, Atlanta, GA.

Devitt, A. J., Bawarshi, A., & Reiff, M. J. (2003). Materiality and genre in the study of discourse communities. *College English, 65*(5), 541–558.

Dietel-McLaughlin, E. (2009, January). Remediating democracy: Irreverent composition and the vernacular rhetorics of Web 2.0. *Computers and Composition Online: Special Web 2.0 Edition.* Retrieved from www.bgsu.edu/cconline/Dietel/Remediating%20Democracy.pdf

Dunbar, K. (1995). How scientists really reason: Scientific reasoning in real-world laboratories. In R.J. Sternberg & J. Davidson (Eds.) *Mechanisms of insight* (pp. 365–395). Cambridge: MIT Press.

Dunbar, K. (1999). Science. In M. Runco & S. R. Pritzker (Eds.), *Encyclopedia of creativity, Vol. 2* (pp. 525–532). San Diego: Academic Press.

Elsevier. (n.d.). *Reviewer guidelines.* Retrieved from www.elsevier.com/reviewers/reviewer-guidelines

Fairclough, N. (1992). *Discourse and social change.* Cambridge, U.K.: Polity Press.

Fairclough, N. (2006). *Language and globalization.* New York: Routledge.

Foucault, M. (1982). The order of discourse. In M. Shapiro (Ed.), *Language and politics* (pp. 108–138). London: Blackwell.

Freadman, A. (1987). Anyone for tennis? In I. Reid (Ed.), *The place of genre in learning: Current debates* (pp. 91–124). Geelong, Australia: Deakin University, Centre for Studies in Literary Education.

Freedman, A. (1993). Show and tell? The role of explicit teaching in the learning of new genres. *Research in the Teaching of English, 27*(3), 222–251.

Frye, N. (1957). *Anatomy of criticism.* Princeton, NJ: Princeton University Press.

Gardner, H. (1993). *Creating minds.* New York: Basic Books.

Gebhard, M., & Harman, R. (2011). Reconsidering genre theory in K–12 schools: A response to school reforms in the United States. *Journal of Second Language Writing, 20*(1), 45–55.

Geertz, C. (2000). *Available light: Anthropological reflections on philosophical topics.* Princeton, NJ: Princeton University Press.

Gentil, G. (2011). A biliteracy agenda for genre research. *Journal of Second Language Writing, 20,* 6–23.

Gentil, G. (in press). Multilingualism as a resource. In J. I. Liontas (Ed.), *The TESOL encyclopedia of English language teaching.* Walden, MA: Wiley.

Gentil, G., & Séror, J. (2014). Canada has two official languages—Or does it? Case studies of Canadian scholars' language choices and practices in disseminating knowledge. *Journal of English for Academic Purposes, 13,* 17–30.

Giltrow, J., & Stein, D. (2009a). Genres in the internet: Innovation, evolution, and genre theory. In J. Giltrow & D. Stein (Eds.), *Genres in the internet: Issues in the theory of genre* (pp. 1–25). Philadelphia: John Benjamins.

Giltrow, J., & Stein, D. (2009b). *Genres in the internet: Issues in the theory of genre.* Philadelphia: John Benjamins.

Gladwell, M. (2000). *The tipping point: How little things can make a big difference.* New York: Little, Brown and Company.

Goodwin-Jones, R. (2012). Digital video revisited: Storytelling, conferencing, remixing. *Language Learning and Technology, 16*(1), 1–9.

Greenall, A. K. (2009). Towards a new theory of flouting. *Journal of Pragmatics, 41,* 2295–2311.

Grice, H. P. (1975). Logic and conversation. In P. Cole & J. L. Morgan (Eds.), *Syntax and semantics, Volume 3: Speech arts* (pp. 41–58). New York: Academic Press.

Grice, H. P. (1989). *Studies in the way of words.* Cambridge, MA: Harvard University Press.

Guetzkow, J., Lamont, M., & Mallard, G. (2004). What is originality in the humanities and social sciences? *American Sociological Review, 69,* 190–212.

Hafner, C. A. (2013). Digital composition in a second or foreign language. *TESOL Quarterly, 47*(4), 830–834.

Hamilton, M., & Pitt, K. (2009). Creativity in academic writing: Escaping from the straitjacket of genre? In A. Carter, T. Lillis, & S. Parkin (Eds.), *Why writing matters: Issues of access and identity in writing research and pedagogy* (pp. 61–79). Philadelphia: John Benjamins.

Harklau, L. (2000). From the 'good kids' to the 'worst': Representations of English language learners across educational settings. *TESOL Quarterly, 34*(1), 35–67.

Heng Hartse, J., & Kubota, R. (2014). Pluralizing English? Variation in high-stakes academic texts and challenges of copyediting. *Journal of Second Language Writing, 24,* 71–82.

Herrington, A. J. (1985). Writing in academic settings: A study of the contexts for writing in two college chemical engineering courses. *Research in the Teaching of English, 19*(4), 331–361.

Herrington, A. J. (1988). Teaching, writing, and learning: A naturalistic study of writing in an undergraduate literature course. In D. A. Jolliffe (Ed.), *Advances in writing research, Vol. 2: Writing in academic disciplines* (pp. 133–166). Norwood, NJ: Ablex.

Hipschman, R. (n.d.). *How SETI@home works.* Retrieved from www.seticlassic.ssl.berkeley.edu/about_seti/about_seti_at_home_1.html

Horner, B., Lu, M.-Z., Royster, J. J., & Trimbur, J. (2011). Language difference in writing: Toward a translingual approach. *College English, 73*(3), 303–321.

Hyland, K. (2000). *Disciplinary discourses: Social interactions in academic writing.* London: Longman.

Hyland, K. (2004). *Genre and second language writing.* Ann Arbor: University of Michigan Press.

Hyland, K. (2007). Genre pedagogy: Language, literacy, and L2 writing instruction. *Journal of Second Language Writing, 16,* 148–164.

Hyland, K. (2008). 'Small bits of textual material': A discourse analysis of Swales' writing. *English for Specific Purposes, 27*(2), 143–160.

Hyland, K. (2010). Community and individuality: Performing identity in applied linguistics. *Written Communication, 27*(2), 159–188.

Hyland, K. (2012). *Disciplinary identities: Individuality and community in academic discourse.* Cambridge, U.K.: Cambridge University Press.

Hyon, S. (2008). Convention and inventiveness in an occluded academic genre: A case study of retention-promotion-tenure reports. *English for Specific Purposes, 27*(2), 175–192.

Hyon, S. (2015). Genre play: Moving students from formulaic and complex academic writing. In M. Roberge, K. Losey, & M. Wald (Eds.), *Teaching U.S.-educated multilingual writers* (pp. 70–107). Ann Arbor: University of Michigan Press.

Institute of International Education. (2011). *Open doors data.* Retrieved from www.iie.org/Research-and-Publications/Open-Doors/Data

Ivanič, R. (1998). *Writing and identity: The discoursal construction of identity in academic writing.* Philadelphia: John Benjamins.

Jaschik, S. (2012, January 12). Dissing the dissertation. *Inside Higher Ed.* Retrieved from www.insidehighered.com/news/2012/01/09/mla-considers-radical-changes-dissertation

Jiguet, F., Devictor, V., Julliard, R., & Couvet, D. (2012). French citizens monitoring ordinary birds provide tools for conservation and ecological sciences. *Acta Oecologica, 48,* 58–66.

Johns, A. M. (1997). *Text, role, and context: Developing academic literacies.* New York: Cambridge University Press.

Johns, A. M. (2002a). Destabilizing and enriching novice students' genre theories. In A. M. Johns (Ed.), *Genre in the classroom: Multiple perspectives* (pp. 237–246). Mahwah, NJ: Lawrence Erlbaum.

Johns, A. M. (Ed.) (2002b). *Genre in the classroom: Multiple perspectives.* Mahwah, NJ: Lawrence Erlbaum.

Johns, A. M. (2008). Genre awareness for the novice academic student: An ongoing quest. *Language Teaching, 41*(2), 237–252.

Johns, A. M. (2011). The future of genre in L2 writing: Fundamental, but contested, instructional decisions. *Journal of Second Language Writing, 20,* 56–88.

Johns, A. M., Bawarshi, A., Coe, R. M., Hyland, K., Paltridge, B., Reiff, M. J., & Tardy, C. M. (2006). Crossing the boundaries of genre studies: Commentaries by experts. *Journal of Second Language Writing, 15,* 234–249.

Jones, R. H. (2010). Creativity and discourse. *World Englishes, 29*(4), 467–480.

Kachru, B. B. (1985). The bilinguals' creativity. *Annual Review of Applied Linguistics, 6,* 20–33.

Kachru, B. B. (1986). *The alchemy of English: The spread, functions, and models of non-native Englishes.* Champaign: University of Illinois Press.

Kachru, B. B. (1988). The spread of English and sacred linguistic cows. In P. Lowenberg (Ed.), *Georgetown University Roundtable on Languages and Linguistics 1987* (pp. 207–228). Washington, DC: Georgetown University Press.

Kachru, Y. (1997). Cultural meaning and contrastive rhetoric in English education. *World Englishes, 16*(3), 337–350.

Kamberelis, G. (1995). Genre as institutionally informed social practice. *Journal of Contemporary Legal Issues, 6*, 115–171.

Kaufer, D. S., & Geisler, C. (1989). Novelty in academic writing. *Written Communication, 6*(3), 286–311.

Kill, M. (2008). *Challenging communication: A genre theory of innovative uptake.* Unpublished doctoral dissertation, University of Washington.

Kopelson, K. (2014). On the politics of not paying attention (and the resistance of resistance). In B. Horner & K. Kopelson (Eds.), *Reworking English in rhetoric and composition: Global interrogations, local interventions* (pp. 207–218). Carbondale: Southern Illinois University Press.

Korpela, E. J., Anderson, D. P., Bankay, R., Cobb, J., Howard, A., Lebofsky, M., Siemion, A. P. V., von Korff, J., & Werthimer, D. (2011, August). *Status of the UC-Berkeley SETI efforts* (arXiv: 1108.3134v1). Available from www.setiathome.berkeley.edu

Kozbelt, A., Beghetto, R. A., & Runco, M. A. (2010). Theories of creativity. In J. C. Kaufman & R. J. Sternberg (Eds.), *The Cambridge handbook of creativity* (pp. 20–47). New York: Cambridge University Press.

Kramsch, C. (2001). Language, culture, and voice in the teaching of English as a foreign language. *NovELTy: A Journal of English Language Teaching and Cultural Studies in Hungary, 8*(1), 4–21.

Kramsch, C., & Steffensen, S. V. (2008). Ecological perspectives on second language acquisition and socialization. In P. A. Duff & N. H. Hornberger (Eds.), *Encyclopedia of language and education, Vol. 8* (2nd ed.) (pp. 17–28). New York: Springer.

Kramsch, C., & Sullivan, P. (1996). Appropriate pedagogy. *ELT Journal, 50*(3), 199–212.

Kress, G. (1987). Genre in a social theory of language: A reply to John Dixon. In I. Reid (Ed.), *The place of genre in learning: Current debates* (pp. 35–45). Geelong, Australia: Deakin University Press.

Kress, G. (1993). Genre as social process. In B. Cope & M. Kalantzis (Eds.), *The powers of literacy: A genre approach to teaching writing* (pp. 22–37). Pittsburgh, PA: University of Pittsburgh Press.

Kress, G. (1999). Genre and the changing contexts for English language arts. *Language Arts, 76*, 461–469.

Kubota, R. (2003). Striving for original voice in publication? A critical reflection. In C. P. Casanave & S. Vandrick (Eds.), *Writing for scholarly publication: Behind the scenes in language education* (pp. 61–69). Mahwah, NJ: Lawrence Erlbaum.

Kubota, R. (2012). The politics of EIL: Toward border-crossing communication in and beyond English. In A. Matsuda (Ed.), *Principles and practices of teaching English as an international language* (pp. 55–69). Bristol, U.K.: Multilingual Matters.

Kuteeva, M. (2013). Graduate learners' approaches to genre-analysis tasks: Variations across and within four disciplines. *English for Specific Purposes, 32*, 84–96.

Lamont, M. (2009). *How professors think: Inside the curious world of academic judgment*. Cambridge, MA: Harvard University Press.

Lantolf, J. (1997). The function of language play in the acquisition of L2 Spanish. In W. Glass & A.T. Leroux-Perez (Eds.), *Contemporary perspectives on the acquisition of Spanish* (pp. 3–24). Somerville, MA: Cascadilla Press.

Laquintano, T. (2010). Sustained authorship: Digital writing, self-publishing, and the ebook. *Written Communication, 27*(4), 469–493.

Larsen-Freeman, D. (1997). Chaos/complexity science and second language acquisition. *Applied Linguistics, 18*(2), 141–165.

Le Ha, P. (2009). Strategic, passionate, but academic. *Journal of English for Academic Purposes, 8*(2), 134–146.

Leki, I. (1995). Coping strategies of ESL students in writing tasks across the curriculum. *TESOL Quarterly, 29*(2), 235–260.

Lemke, J. L. (1993). Discourse, dynamics, and social change. *Cultural Dynamics, 6*(1), 243–275.

Lemke, J. L. (1995). *Textual politics: Discourse and social dynamics*. Bristol, PA: Taylor & Francis.

Lemke, J. L. (2000). Across the scales of time: Artifacts, activities, and meanings in ecosocial systems. *Mind, Culture, and Activity, 7*(4), 273–290.

Li, Y. (2007). Shaping Chinese novice scientists' manuscripts for publication. *Journal of Second Language Writing, 16*, 100–117.

Limerick, P. N. (1993, October 31). Dancing with professors: The trouble with academic prose. *New York Times*, pp. A3, A23.

Lu, M.-Z. (1994). Professing multiculturalism: The politics of style in the contact zone. *College Composition and Communication, 45*(4), 442–458.

Lubart, T. (2010). Cross-cultural perspectives on creativity. In J. C. Kaufman & R. J. Sternberg (Eds.), *The Cambridge handbook of creativity* (pp. 265–278). New York: Cambridge University Press.

Luke, A. (1996). Genres of power? Literacy education and the production of capital. In R. Hasan & G. Williams (Eds.), *Literacy in Society* (pp. 308–338). London: Longman.

Mao, L. (2002). Re-clustering traditional academic discourse: Alternating with Confucian discourse. In C. Schroeder, H. Fox, & P. Bizzell (Eds.), *ALT/DIS: Alternative discourses and the academy* (pp. 112–125). Portsmouth, NH: Boynton/Cook Heinemann.

Martin, J. R. (2002). A universe of meaning—How many practices? In A. M. Johns (Ed.), *Genre in the classroom: Multiple perspectives* (pp. 269–278). Mahwah, NJ: Lawrence Erlbaum.

Matsuda, A. (2012a). Introduction: Teaching English as an international language. In A. Matsuda (Ed.), *Principles and practices of teaching English as an international language* (pp. 1–14). Bristol, U.K.: Multilingual Matters.

Matsuda, A. (Ed.) (2012b). *Principles and practices of teaching English as an international language*. Bristol, U.K.: Multilingual Matters.

Matsuda, A., & Matsuda, P. K. (2010). World Englishes and the teaching of writing. *TESOL Quarterly, 44*(2), 369–374.

Matsuda, A., & Matsuda, P. K. (2011). Globalizing writing studies: The case of U.S. technical communication textbooks. *Written Communication, 28,* 172–192.

Matsuda, P. K. (2001). Voice in Japanese written discourse: Implications for second language writing. *Journal of Second Language Writing, 10,* 35–53.

Matsuda, P. K. (2002). Alternative discourses: A synthesis. In C. Schroeder, H. Fox, & P. Bizzell (Eds.), *ALT/DIS: Alternative discourses and the academy* (pp. 191–196). Portsmouth, NH: Boynton/Cook Heinemann.

Matsuda, P. K. (2006). The myth of linguistic homogeneity in U.S. college composition. *College Composition and Communication, 68*(6), 637–651.

Matsuda, P. K. (2013). It's the wild west out there: A new linguistic frontier in U.S. college composition. In A. S. Canagarajah (Ed.), *Literacy as translingual practice: Between communities and classrooms* (pp. 128–138). London: Routledge.

Matsuda, P. K. (2015). Identity in written discourse. *Annual Review of Applied Linguistics, 35,* 140–159.

Matsuda, P. K., & Atkinson, D. (2008). A conversation on contrastive rhetoric: Dwight Atkinson and Paul Kei Matsuda talk about issues, conceptualizations, and the future of contrastive rhetoric. In U. Connor, E. Nagelhout, & W. Rozycki (Eds.), *Contrastive rhetoric: Reaching to intercultural rhetoric* (pp. 277–298). Amsterdam: John Benjamins.

Matsuda, P. K., & Tardy, C. M. (2007). Voice in academic writing: The rhetorical construction of author identity in blind manuscript review. *English for Specific Purposes, 26,* 235–249.

Maurer, E. G. (2009). "Working consensus" and the rhetorical situation: The homeless blog's negotiation of public meta-genre. In J. Giltrow & D. Stein (Eds.), *Genres in the internet: Issues in the theory of genre* (pp. 113–142). Philadelphia: John Benjamins.

Maybin, J., & Swann, J. (2007). Everyday creativity in language: Textuality, contextuality, and critique. *Applied Linguistics, 28*(4), 497–517.

Mayer, R. E. (1999). Fifty years of creativity research. In R. J. Sternberg (Ed.), *Handbook of creativity* (pp. 449–460). New York: Cambridge University Press.

Meadows, D. H. (2008). *Thinking in systems: A primer.* White River Junction, VT: Chelsea Green.

Michaels, S. (2014, September 29). Scientists sneak Bob Dylan lyrics into articles as part of long-running bet. *The Guardian*. Retrieved from www. theguardian.com/music/2014/sep/29/swedish-cientists-bet-bob-dylan-lyrics-research-papers

Miller, C. R. (1984). Genre as social action. *Quarterly Journal of Speech, 70*, 151–167.

Miller, C. R., & Shepherd, D. (2004). Blogging as social action: A genre analysis of the weblog. In L.J. Gurak, S. Antonijevic, L. Johnson, C. Ratliff, & J. Reyman (Eds.), *Into the blogosphere: Rhetoric, community, and culture of weblogs*. Retrieved from www.blog.lib.umn.edu/blogosphere/blogging_as_social_action_a_genre_analysis_of_the_weblog.html

Miller, J. R., & Tewksbury, R. (2001). *Extreme methods: Innovative approaches to social science research*. Boston: Allyn & Bacon.

Miner, H. (1956). Body ritual among the Nacirema. *American Anthropologist, 58*(3), 503–507.

Modern Language Association. (2006). Report of the MLA task force on evaluating scholarship for tenure and promotion. Retrieved from www.mla.org/pdf/taskforcereport0608.pdf

Modern Language Association. (2015). Back on track: Connecting with former graduate students. *MLA Newsletter, 47*(1), 5.

Myles, D., & Artemeva, N. (2014, November). *An examination of students' perceptions of the role of prior genre knowledge in the English for academic purposes classroom*. Paper presented at the Symposium on Second Language Writing, Tempe, AZ.

Nash, R. J. (2004). *Liberating scholarly writing: The power of personal narrative*. New York: Teachers College Press.

Negretti, R., & Kuteeva, M. (2011). Fostering metacognitive genre awareness in L2 academic reading and writing: A case study of pre-service English teachers. *Journal of Second Language Writing, 20*, 95–110.

Norvig, P. (n.d.). *The Gettysburg PowerPoint presentation*. Retrieved from www.norvig.com/Gettysburg/

Ortner, S. B. (1996). *Making gender: The politics and erotics of culture*. Boston: Beacon Press.

Paltridge, B. (1997). *Genre, frames and writing in research settings*. Philadelphia: John Benjamins.

Paltridge, B. (2001). *Genre and the language learning classroom*. Ann Arbor: University of Michigan Press.

Paul, D., Charney, D., & Kendall, A. (2001). Moving beyond the moment: Reception studies in the rhetoric of science. *Journal of Business and Technical Communication, 15*(3), 372–399.

Pennycook, A. (2007). 'The rotation gets thick. The constraints get thin': Creativity, recontextualization, and difference. *Applied Linguistics, 28*(4), 579–596.

Pennycook, A. (2010). *Language as a local practice.* New York: Routledge.

Pennycook, A. (2012). *Language and mobility: Unexpected places.* Bristol, U.K.: Multilingual Matters.

Perryman-Clark, S., Kirkland, D. E., & Jackson, A. (Eds.) (2014). *Students' right to their own language: A critical sourcebook.* Boston: Bedford/St. Martin's.

Platt, J. R. (1964). Strong inference. *Science, 146*(3642), 347–353.

Pomerantz, A., & Bell, N. D. (2007). Learning to play, playing to learn: FL learners as multicompetent language users. *Applied Linguistics, 28*(4), 556–578.

Pope, R. (2005). *Creativity: Theory, history, practice.* New York: Routledge.

Prior, P. A. (1998). *Writing/disciplinarity: A sociohistoric account of literate activity in the academy.* Mahwah, NJ: Lawrence Erlbaum Associates.

Prior, P. A. (2001). Voices in text, mind, and society: Sociohistoric accounts of discourse acquisition and use. *Journal of Second Language Writing, 10,* 55–81.

Prior, P. A. (2009). From speech genres to mediated multimodal genre systems: Bahktin, Voloshinov, and the question of writing. In C. Bazerman, A. Bonini, & D. Figueiredo (Eds.), *Genre in a changing world* (pp. 17–34). West Lafayette, IN: Parlor Press.

Reiff, M. J., & Bawarshi, A. (2011). Tracing discursive resources: How students use prior genre knowledge to negotiate new writing contexts in first-year composition. *Written Communication, 28*(3), 312–337.

Richards, E., & Ashmore, M. (1996). More sauce please! The politics of SSK: Neutrality, commitment and beyond. *Social Studies of Science, 26,* 219–228.

Rose, D., & Martin, J. R. (2012). *Learning to write, reading to learn: Genre, knowledge and pedagogy in the Sydney School.* Bristol, CT: Equinox.

Rozycki, W., & Johnson, N. H. (2013). Non-canonical grammar in best paper award winners in engineering. *English for Specific Purposes, 32,* 157–169.

Russell, D. H. (1997). Rethinking genre in school and society: An activity theory analysis. *Written Communication, 14,* 504–554.

Sand-Jensen, K. (2007). How to write consistently boring scientific literature. *Oikos, 116,* 723–727.

Saussure, F. de (1983). *Course in general linguistics* (C. Bally & A. Sechehaye, Eds., R. Harris, Trans.). LaSalle, IL: Open Court.

Sawyer, K. (2012). *Explaining creativity: The science of human innovation* (2nd ed.). New York: Oxford University Press.

Schroeder, C., Fox, H., & Bizzell, P. (Eds.) (2002). *ALT DIS: Alternative discourses and the academy.* Portsmouth, NH: Boynton/Cook Heinemann.

Schryer, C. F. (2011, February). *Genre as generative.* Paper presented at Writing and Rhetoric Across Borders Conference, Fairfax, VA.

Schutz, A., & Luckmann, T. (1973). *The structures of the life-world*. Evanston, IL: Northwestern University Press.

Smitherman, G. (1976). Soul 'n style. *English Journal, 63*(3), 14–15.

Smitherman, G. (2003). The historical struggle for language rights in CCCC. In G. Smitherman & V. Villanueva (Eds.), *Language diversity in the classroom: From intention to practice* (pp. 7–39). Urbana, IL: NCTE.

Smitherman, G., & Villanueva, V. (Eds.) (2003). *Language diversity in the classroom: From intention to practice*. Urbana, IL: NCTE.

Sokal, A. (1996a, May/June). A physicist experiments with cultural studies. *Lingua Franca*, 62–64.

Sokal, A. (1996b). Transgressing the boundaries: Towards a transformative hermeneutics of quantum gravity. *Social Text, 46/47*, 217–252.

Sokal, A. (2000). Revelation: A physicist experiments with cultural studies. In The Editors of *Lingua Franca* (Eds.), *The Sokal hoax: The sham that shook the academy* (pp. 49–53). Lincoln: University of Nebraska Press.

Sokal, A. (2008). *Beyond the hoax: Science, philosophy and culture*. Oxford, U.K.: Oxford University Press.

Starfield, S., & Ravelli, L. J. (2006). 'The writing of this thesis was a process that I could not explore with the positivistic detachment of the classical sociologist': Self and structure in *New Humanities* research theses. *Journal of English for Academic Purposes, 5*, 222–243.

Swales, J. M. (1985). English language papers and authors' first language: Preliminary explorations. *Scientometrics, 8*(1–2), 91–101.

Swales, J. M. (1990). *Genre analysis: English in academic and research settings*. Cambridge, U.K.: Cambridge University Press.

Swales, J. M. (1993). Genre and engagement. *La Revue Belge de Philologic et l'histoire, 71*, 687–698.

Swales, J. M. (1997). English as *Tyrannosaurus rex*. *World Englishes, 16*(3), 373–382.

Swales, J. M. (1998). *Other floors, other voices: A textography of a small university building*. Mahwah, NJ: Lawrence Erlbaum.

Swales, J. M. (2004). *Research genres: Explorations and applications*. Cambridge, U.K.: Cambridge University Press.

Swales, J. M. (2009). *Incidents in an educational life: A memoir (of sorts)*. Ann Arbor: University of Michigan Press.

Swales, J. M., & Leeder, C. (2012). A reception study of the articles published in *English for Specific Purposes* from 1990–1999. *English for Specific Purposes, 31*, 137–146.

Swann, J., Pope, R., & Carter, R. (2011). *Creativity in language and literature: The state of the art*. New York: Palgrave Macmillan.

Sword, H. (2009). Writing higher education differently: A manifesto on style. *Studies in Higher Education, 34*(3), 319–336.

Sykes, J. M., & Reinhardt, J. (2012). *Language at play: Digital games in second and foreign language teaching and learning.* New York: Pearson.

Tardy, C. M. (2003). A genre system view of the funding of academic research. *Written Communication, 20*(1), 7–36.

Tardy, C. M. (2005). Expressions of disciplinarity and individuality in a multi-modal genre. *Computers and Composition, 22*(3), 319–336.

Tardy, C. M. (2006). Researching first and second language genre learning: A comparative review and a look ahead. *Journal of Second Language Writing, 15*(2), 79–101.

Tardy, C. M. (2009). *Building genre knowledge.* West Lafayette, IN: Parlor Press.

Tardy, C. M. (2012a). Current conceptions of voice. In K. Hyland & C. S. Guinda (Eds.), *Stance and voice in academic discourse* (pp. 34–48). New York: Palgrave Macmillan.

Tardy, C. M. (2012b). Voice construction, assessment, and extra-textual identity. *Research in the Teaching of English, 47*(1), 64–99.

Tardy, C. M. (in press). Voice and identity. In R. M. Manchón & P. K. Matsuda (Eds.), *Handbook of second and foreign language writing.* Berlin: Mouton de Gruyter.

Tardy, C. M. & Matsuda, P. K. (2009). The construction of author voice by editorial board members. *Written Communication, 26,* 32–52.

Tarone, E. (2000). Getting serious about language play: Language play, inter-language variation and second language acquisition. In B. Swierzbein, F. Morris, M. Anderson, C. Klee, & E. Tarone (Eds.), *Social and cognitive factors in second language acquisition* (pp. 31–54). Somerville, CA: Cascadilla Press.

Tarone, E. (2002). Frequency effects, noticing, and creativity: Factors in a variationist interlanguage framework. *SSLA, 24,* 287–296.

Tawake, S. (2003). Bilinguals' creativity: Patricia Grace and Maori cultural context. *World Englishes, 22*(1), 45–55.

Thaiss, C., & Zawacki, T. M. (2006). *Engaged writers and dynamic disciplines: Research on the academic writing life.* Portsmouth, NH: Boynton/Cook Heinemann.

University of Queensland. (n.d.). *Three minute thesis.* Retrieved from www.threeminutethesis.org

van Dam, J. (2002). Ritual, face, and play in a first English lesson: Bootstrapping a classroom culture. In C. Kramsch (Ed.), *Language acquisition and language socialization: Ecological perspectives* (pp. 237–265). New York: Continuum.

Vandrick, S. (2009). *Interrogating privilege: Reflections of a second language educator.* Ann Arbor: University of Michigan Press.

Vandrick, S., & Casanave, C. P. (2014, March). *Scholarly memoirs in TESOL: Exemplars, connections, and contributions.* Paper presented at TESOL, Portland, OR.

Villanueva, V. (1993). *Bootstraps: From an American academic of color*. Urbana, IL: NCTE.

Waring, H. Z. (2013). Doing being playful in the second language classroom. *Applied Linguistics, 34*(2), 191–210.

Warner, C. N. (2004). It's just a game, right? Types of play in foreign language CMC. *Language, Learning & Technology, 8*(2), 69–87.

Widdowson, H. G. (2008). Language creativity and the poetic function. A response to Swann and Maybin (2007). *Applied Linguistics, 29*(3), 503–508.

Wilder, L. (2002). "Get comfortable with uncertainty": A study of the conventional values of literary analysis in an undergraduate literature course. *Written Communication, 19*(1), 175–221.

Wittgenstein, L. (1968). *Philosophical investigations* (G. E. M. Anscombe, Trans.). Oxford, U.K.: Blackwell.

Yajun, J., & Chenggang, Z. (2006). World Englishes and contrastive rhetoric. *English Today, 22*(2), 11–22.

You, X. (2011). Chinese white-collar workers and multilingual creativity in the diaspora. *World Englishes, 30*(3), 409–427.

Young, V. A., & Martinez, A. Y. (Eds.) (2011). *Code-meshing as world English: Pedagogy, policy, performance*. Urbana, IL: NCTE.

Zooniverse. Tutorial. (2011). In *Whale FM*. Retrieved from www.whale.fm/tutorial

Index